T0317161

THE LAW OF PRESIDENTIAL IMPEACHMENT

The Law of
Presidential Impeachment

A GUIDE FOR THE ENGAGED CITIZEN

Michael J. Gerhardt

NEW YORK UNIVERSITY PRESS

New York

NEW YORK UNIVERSITY PRESS
New York
www.nyupress.org

Please contact the Library of Congress for Cataloging-in-Publication data.
ISBN: 9781479824694 (hardback)
ISBN: 9781479824724 (library ebook)
ISBN: 9781479824717 (consumer ebook)

This book is printed on acid-free paper, and its binding materials are chosen
for strength and durability. We strive to use environmentally responsible
suppliers and materials to the greatest extent possible in publishing
our books.

Manufactured in the United States of America

10 9 8 7 6 5 4 3 2 1

Also available as an ebook

To Senator Patrick J. Leahy—

In appreciation for his lifetime of public service

and allowing me to be a part of the Senate

and the Constitution in action.

The President Is of a Very Different Nature from a Monarch. He is to be Personally Responsible for Any Abuse of the Great Trust Placed in Him.

—James Iredell (1788)

No man is above the law and no man is below, nor do we ask for any man's permission when we require him to obey it. Obedience to the law is demanded as a right; not asked for as a favor.

—President Theodore Roosevelt (1903)

My faith in the Constitution is whole; it is complete; it is total. And I am not going to sit here and be an idle spectator to the diminution, the subversion, the destruction, of the Constitution.

—Rep. Barbara Jordan (1974)

CONTENTS

Almost every generation in America has discovered an unsettling truth about our Constitution: the mechanisms for holding presidents accountable for their misconduct are far from perfect. Presidents do engage in misconduct—from obstruction of justice to lying to the American people to using their powers to benefit themselves financially and to harass their political enemies—but none has ever been ousted from office through impeachment. Despite the four times presidents have faced impeachment proceedings since 1974, including the two most recent against Donald Trump, there have been remarkably few if any lasting lessons learned by Congress, by the media, and by the public. With each new attempt to oust a president under the Constitution, it seems the nation needs a refresher course on the law of presidential impeachment.

There are many likely causes for this predicament. The constitutionally required two-thirds threshold in the Senate for removing an impeached official makes ousting presidents practically impossible. So long as the members of the president's party stick together in opposition to any impeachment attempt, they can block conviction and removal of a president, assuming their party holds more than a third of the seats in the Senate. The 24-hour news cycle has widened the breach dividing Americans and corrupted political discourse. Unlike any other impeachable official in the United States, presidents command an extensive branch of government, one that is devoted to keeping him in office.

For much of the American public, political leadership, and media, the fundamental issue posed by a presidential impeachment—whether the president has committed misconduct sufficiently serious as to warrant ouster from office by Congress—has turned less on the merits and more on the political party to which the impeached president belongs. Alexander Hamilton had warned in 1788 that "[p]rosecutions of impeachments will seldom fail to agitate the passions of the whole community," but Congresswoman Barbara Jordan advised the nation in 1974 that "[i]t is reason, not passion, which must guide our deliberations, guide our debate, and guide our decision."[1] Her admonition has been lost on many, as Americans' party fealty, exacerbated by tribalism and the advent of infotainment on the internet, has weakened confidence in public institutions and in impeachment as a serious check against presidential misconduct.

These are just some of the costs resulting from the growing phenomenon of disinformation in America, that is, the proliferation of misleading or false narratives that challenge, if not substitute for, a sound, evenhanded understanding of the federal impeachment process. In this country, we do not have a Republican or a Democratic Constitution. We do not (or should not) have a Constitution that works differently depending on the political party of the incumbent president. We have an *American* Constitution, a document that is supposed to apply to every president the same way and thereby ensure that no president is above the law.

Having devoted more than thirty years to studying, consulting, analyzing, and testifying on the federal impeachment process, my purpose is to dispel the disinformation mischaracterizing the constitutional mechanisms, particularly regarding impeachment, for holding presidents accountable for their misconduct. I aim to provide a succinct, evenhanded, coherent analysis of the law of presidential impeachment, one that, I hope, will withstand the test of time.

Let's begin by stating the matter clearly: Certain officeholders may be subject to impeachment for treason, bribery, and serious abuses of power; impeachment is designed to address serious misconduct that is not easily (or perhaps ever) redressable through legal proceedings such as civil or criminal trials; and impeachable offenses require proof of bad or malicious intent *and* a bad act. Context illuminates the gravity of the (mis)conduct: an act that might appear innocuous in one setting might seriously injure the republic in another. A president's lies, for example, about the size of the crowd at his inauguration hardly rise to the level of an impeachable offense, but a president who lies to the Senate to secure a treaty's ratification so that he—or a foreign power to whom he is indebted—benefits has damaged and undermined public and international confidence in the integrity of that process.

While many people worry that the constitutional language determining the scope of impeachable offenses—"treason, bribery, and other high crimes and misdemeanors"—is opaque, in fact it is not. The Constitution defines "treason" generally as levying war against the United States or giving aid and comfort to enemies of the United States; "bribery" as either what the framers understood as—or Congress later codified as the felony of—misusing office for personal gain; and "other high crimes and misdemeanors" as serious breaches of the public trust or abuses of power. There was surprising consensus among the framers and ratifiers about the scope of impeachable offenses. And we do not have to look hard to find statements from authoritative figures on the abuses of power qualifying as the grounds for impeachment. For example, Alexander Hamilton explained in *The Federalist Papers* that "[t]he subjects of [the Senate's] jurisdiction [in impeachment trials] are those offenses which proceed from the misconduct of public men [or] from the abuse or violation of some public trust. They are of a nature which may with peculiar propriety be denominated POLITICAL, as they relate chiefly to injuries done immediately to the society itself."[2] Similarly, Justice Joseph Story, in his landmark treatise *Commentaries on the Constitution*, explained that "[s]uch kinds of misdeeds . . . peculiarly injure the commonwealth by the abuse of high trust or office."[3] Moreover, during the ratification process for the Constitution, James Iredell (later appointed to the Supreme Court by President George Washington) explained to his fellow North Carolina delegates that the "occasion for [the impeachment power's] exercise will arise from acts of great injury to the community."[4] After the Constitution was ratified, Justice James Wilson, an important member of the Constitutional Convention and the Pennsylvania ratifying convention, delivered a public lecture explaining that impeachments are "proceedings of a political nature . . . confined to political characters, to political crimes and misdemeanors, and to political punishments."[5]

Even these basic elements of impeachment have been obscured or distorted as presidents have used the bully pulpit and their administrations to thwart the threat and sting of impeachment. There is no value in recycling ridiculous, partisan, or cockamamie opinions on the subject spread throughout the internet and in the media. Instead my intention is to help set the record straight as a baseline for anyone interested in developing the correct understanding of the law of presidential impeachment.

In 1974, the eminent constitutional scholar Charles Black wrote an elegant work titled *Impeachment: A Handbook.* It served its purpose and deserved the widespread bipartisan respect it received.[6] Perhaps this book can achieve a similar impact nearly half a century later. Black's keen and often prescient insights have yet to be proven wrong, but recently we have had to confront more issues than he addressed. These include whether a president's repeated failure to comply with congressional subpoenas is a basis for impeachment (I testified before the House Judiciary Committee in 2019 that I believe it is); whether a president's pardoning himself is impeachable; whether it is permissible for Congress to impeach a president after he leaves office; what kinds of process (if any) Congress must follow in presidential impeachment proceedings; and whether the Chief Justice of the United States has anything but ceremonial powers when presiding over presidential impeachment trials. The time is long overdue to explain these and other basic features of the law of presidential impeachment for the American people.

After reviewing why and how the framers chose and the ratifiers approved the constitutional process to address serious presidential misconduct, I analyze each attempt to impeach and oust an American president: Andrew Johnson (1868), Richard Nixon (1974), Bill Clinton (1998), Donald Trump (2019), and Donald Trump again (2021). In analyzing each proceeding, I dispel myths surrounding and clarify the law guiding impeachment. Because of presidential access to the bully pulpit, the arguments made in defense tend to obscure the law. Presidents and their defenders have frequently asserted deeply flawed conceptions of impeachment to facilitate their primary objective: to elude any sanction resulting from the impeachment process. For example, Andrew Johnson assembled one of the most elite legal teams at the time for his defense, but they argued that impeachments must be actual crimes, which is the same flawed argument employed on behalf of Richard Nixon and later Donald Trump when they faced the threat of impeachment and removal from office. Bill Clinton successfully defended himself on the ground that not all crimes are impeachable, a valid but incomplete statement of the law of impeachment.

Justice Joseph Story explained in his landmark commentaries that the nature of impeachable offenses made it impossible to codify, ahead of time, a list of all the (mis)deeds for which presidents might be impeached. The fact that we have had only four seriously attempted presidential impeachments confirms his point. We have had too few such proceedings to concoct a code of all the offenses for which presidents may be impeached, convicted, and removed from office.

While presidents have incentives to narrow the scope of impeachable misconduct to exclude their own activities, the law has several safeguards (such as requiring senators to be on oath and affirmation and requiring at least two-thirds approval of the Senate for conviction and removal) that effectively guard against the misuse of the impeachment process. It is safe to say that, in America, the process has been underutilized rather than abused for fear of transforming our system of law from a constitutional republic into a parliamentary system, especially popular in Great Britain. The fear of upending a presidential election is entirely misplaced; the fact is that impeachment was created precisely to create that option when presidents seriously abuse their powers.

The president oversees the executive branch, which has (not surprisingly) often rallied against a sitting president's potential liability for legal and constitutional violations. Beginning in the Nixon administration and extending to both the Clinton and Trump administrations, the Justice Department has maintained the practice of treating sitting presidents as being immune to criminal investigations and prosecutions. This position has been open to question; after all, the lawyers asserting that claim work for the president. They have personal and institutional interests in backing the myth of a president's entitlement to some special immunity that is not available to the leaders of other branches of the federal government.

To arrive at any such conclusion requires ignoring crucial differences between the British system of impeachment at or around the time of the founding and our own Constitution. The American colonists were so incensed that the king of England was the only official not subject to impeachment that it provoked them to declare independence. In fact, the grounds for this were set forth as impeachment articles in the Declaration of Independence. Eventually they would create the United States Constitution, in which the chief executive is not a monarch but an elected official who assumes office subject to impeachment for "treason, bribery, and other high crimes or misdemeanors." Any notion that presidents are not subject to criminal process effectively places them above the law while they hold office; in fact that is the point of the sort of immunity that defenders of the president claim.

But claiming such immunity from accountability is contrary to everything we know about the law of presidential impeachment. It conflicts with widespread agreement among delegates to the Constitutional Convention and to state ratifying conventions that presidents are not above the law and that they are not kings or monarchs or immune to impeachments or any regular legal processes. In fact, such a claim was rejected by the Supreme Court in *Trump v. Vance*,[7] in which seven justices agreed that sitting presidents may be subject to state criminal investigations and prosecutions. The claim that presidents differ from Supreme Court justices and members of Congress because subjecting them to the criminal process interferes with their ability to run the executive branch discounts the fact that criminal investigations and prosecutions of the Chief Justice, other justices, and congressional members will undoubtedly interfere with their duties. While there is obviously such interference, all three branches will continue to function if their leaders are subjected to criminal process because other leaders will take up the slack. The associate justices can ensure that the Court will continue to operate, congressional leaders substitute for each other all the time when one or more of them are dealing with a personal issue or health crisis, and the vice president and cabinet are fully capable of substituting for a president who cannot bring himself to focus on anything other than his own legal troubles.

Only one American president who faced serious threat of impeachment actually acknowledged an accurate understanding of impeachable offenses as reaching misconduct that is not subject to legal process. Richard Nixon resigned rather than face the certitude of impeachment by the House and conviction and removal by the Senate for a criminal offense (obstruction of justice), for refusing to comply with legislative subpoenas (for which there are various legal remedies), and for ordering the heads of three federal agencies to harass his political enemies (not a criminal offense). These facts are sometimes met by arguments that abuse of power is not impeachable because it is not a crime. Such a claim is counter to everything we know about impeachment.

While it is true that abusing power is rarely a crime for which a president could go to prison, it is a dangerous myth that abuse of power is not a violation of some important law. Abuse of power in fact entails deviating from the proper scope of constitutional authority given to the president, and breaching that boundary violates the Constitution, the supreme law of the land. If abuses of power are not impeachable, then we run into a huge problem. There are no civil or criminal remedies for such breaches, and thus presidents would be immune from *ever* being held accountable for abusing their powers. And elections would not act as suitable safeguards because (1) the Constitution gives the Congress, not the public, the discretion to impeach, convict, and remove presidents for committing impeachable offenses and (2) presidents, if they are not impeachable for abusing their powers, would have carte blanche to rig elections since there would be no possible remedy if such efforts were not the basis for impeaching and removing them from office. This book is a road map for understanding, navigating, and reforming the law of presidential impeachments.

In the interests of transparency, I have been influenced by several things in composing this book. First, I believe that the best interpretation of the Constitution is grounded in as many sources of legitimacy as possible, including the text and structure of the Constitution, historical practices (the history of impeachment subsequent to the founding), original meaning (what the framers and ratifiers understood the law of presidential impeachment to be), and an evenhanded assessment of the consequences of different interpretations of the appropriate grounds and procedures for presidential impeachments.

Second, I have studied the impeachment process for decades, beginning with my first article published in 1989 and including two books and other writings on the subject. This book will be my third on the topic. My objective here is the same as it has been for decades: to develop a sound, even-handed understanding of presidential impeachment regardless of its partisan consequences.

I have had the privilege of testifying twice in two different presidential impeachments—once before the House Judiciary Committee as a joint witness (called by both sides) in 1998 and the second time before the same committee in 2019. I also have consulted with many members of Congress on constitutional issues relating to presidential impeachment, including the honor of addressing the entire House of Representatives on that subject a few weeks before I testified during the Clinton impeachment proceedings in 1998. In addition, I have had the privilege of serving as special counsel to the Senate's Presiding Officer in the second trial of Donald Trump in 2021. (Of course, the views expressed in *The Law of Presidential Impeachment* are mine and mine alone.) I also served as an impeachment expert for CNN in both 1998 and 2019. That service, along with my work as the scholar in residence at the National Constitution Center in Philadelphia, reflects my commitment as an educator to speak truth to power on matters relating to presidential impeachment. Just as I have done in my classes for more than three decades, I have worked hard to put aside any partisan attitudes I may have and instead focus primarily on educating as many people as possible about the law of presidential impeachment. I am not a liberal educator or a conservative one, a Democrat or a Republican one. I aim to be a responsible one.

I do not preach partisan politics in my classroom, and I do not preach it here in these pages. Just as Charles Black did in 1974, I aim to explain the law without regard to partisan bias or self-interest. I hope you will agree that I have done this and by doing so have helped to salvage the law of presidential impeachment from the forces of disinformation.

How Impeachment Works

United States Constitution, Article II, section 4:
The President, Vice President and all civil Officers
of the United States, shall be removed from Office
on Impeachment for, and Conviction of, Treason,
Bribery, or other high Crimes and Misdemeanors.*

When the Constitutional Convention convened in Philadelphia on May 25, 1787, the delegates agreed on only a
few matters: One was the need for a new constitution to
establish a chief executive, something lacking in the Articles of Confederation, which for a decade had governed
the operations of the then-existing national government.
In *The Federalist Papers*, Alexander Hamilton explained
that energy in the chief executive was "the leading char-
acteristic of good government."[1] At the same time, the
delegates agreed that this new chief executive would not be
above the law as King George III had been. Instead, they
created a chief executive who would be politically accountable *and* subject to conviction and removal from office for
serious misconduct. The framers had not fought a revolution to break free of the tyrannical King George, only to

turn around almost immediately thereafter and establish a monarch for their new nation.

My objective in this chapter is to explain how these new features in the Constitution, along with several others, provide the constitutional framework for holding presidents accountable for misconduct in office. First, I discuss the distinctive features of impeachment in the Constitution. The constitutional scheme for impeachment differed from the British system in significant ways, which need to be recognized to place the law of presidential impeachment in the United States in its proper context. Second, I survey the Constitution's built-in safeguards against abusing the impeachment power. Next, I address a series of major questions that recur nearly every time presidents face serious threats of impeachment. This discussion should help to dispel several misconceptions about the constitutional mechanism for holding presidents accountable for misconduct. Last, I discuss how the different mechanisms for holding presidents accountable for their misconduct fit together.

I

The impeachment power was fundamental to the founding of America. In the Declaration of Independence, the colonists set forth 27 impeachment articles against the tyrannical King George III. These articles charged King George with various abuses of power, including assertions that he "has dissolved Representative Houses repeatedly, for opposing with manly firmness his invasions on the rights of the people"; "has refused for a long time, after such dissolutions, to cause others to be elected"; "obstructed the Administration of Justice"; "has made judges dependent on his Will"; and "has combined with others to subject us to a jurisdiction foreign to our constitution."[2] Notably, none of these abuses were violations of American or British law at the time, but the Declaration of Independence clearly rests on the understanding that such abuses should have been redressable, or curbed, by some means such as impeachment. Indeed, in the English system, everyone but the king was impeachable, and the monarch, as the embodiment of the law, was above it for all practical purposes. At the risk of being punished for seditious libel, the colonists stood their ground and eventually secured their independence from Great Britain after prevailing in the Revolutionary War in 1783.

Within a decade, Americans had drafted and ratified the new Constitution and formed the first government according to its provisions in 1789. The framers created uniquely American features for the impeachment process that contrasted dramatically with the old British system. First, the framers narrowed the scope of people subject to impeachment to the president, vice president, and "all civil officers" of the United States.[3] Most other people, including private citizens, were not subject to impeachment, in contrast to the practice in England (where private citizens who did not hold official office could in fact be impeached for high treason or other crimes and misdemeanors, though the power was used rarely in such cases).

Next, the framers narrowed the grounds for impeachment from the British practice of allowing impeachment for any act. In the Constitution, the scope of impeachable offenses is limited to treason, bribery, or other high crimes or misdemeanors,[4] language borrowed from several former colonies and British practice, which the British legal historian William Blackstone discussed in his seminal treatise on British law.[5]

Third, in England, Parliament could impose any punishment for impeachment, including death. To be sure, Parliament used its power to punish royal ministers it suspected of being corrupt, but private, non-officeholding citizens were not immune and thus had good reason to worry they would be impeached by Parliament and face harsh punishment, including execution. In contrast, Article I of the United States Constitution (on legislative powers) provides that "judgment in cases of impeachment shall not extend further than to removal from office[] and disqualification to hold and enjoy any office of honor, trust, or profit under the United States."[6] As we will see in later chapters, removal from office is straightforward insofar as Congress and the convicted officials have been concerned, but disqualification has not been quite so straightforward. It has been understood in Congress as barring convicted officials from receiving federal pensions and serving in any federal office, though there is not complete unanimity among scholars and members of Congress on the meaning of "disqualification."

Moreover, Parliament required only a majority of each chamber to impeach someone. In the Constitution, the framers divided the federal impeachment authority between the House and the Senate, and they made that division crystal clear in the Constitution by vesting the House with the "sole power of impeachment"[7] and the Senate with the "sole power to try all impeachments."[8] (These are the only two instances in which the Constitution uses the term "sole.") While a majority in the House could impeach a president, the framers added the safeguard that "no person shall be convicted without the Concurrence of two-thirds of the Members [of the Senate] present."[9]

Whereas there were no special procedures in England for impeachment of officials or citizens, the Constitution established two other safeguards for presidential impeachment trials. In Article I, the Constitution requires that senators, when sitting for presidential impeachment trials, shall do so "on oath or affirmation."[10] Further, Article I provides: "When the president of the United States is tried, the Chief Justice shall preside."[11] Otherwise, Article I, section 5 in pertinent part provides that "each House may determine the rules of its proceedings."[12]

These basic features of the law of presidential impeachment have not changed since the ratification of the Constitution in 1787. Yet some major questions recur: What is the scope of impeachable offenses (requiring defining the terms "other high crimes and misdemeanors")? Why did the framers choose the Congress as the institution to wield impeachment authority? Why did they choose the Chief Justice to preside over presidential impeachment trials? Should presidents be held to the same standards as other impeachable offenses, particularly federal judges, who have been the most common subject of impeachment proceedings? And what procedures if any besides those specified in the Constitution apply in impeachment trials generally or in presidential impeachment trials in particular? I turn to these questions in the discussion below.

II

It is thought that perhaps the most vexing question regarding presidential impeachment is the scope of offenses for which the House may impeach the president and the Senate may convict and remove him from office. While the phrase "other high crimes and misdemeanors" is hardly self-defining, it is not as opaque as many commentators, pundits, and members of Congress insist.

To begin with, "treason" and "bribery," the first two expressly mentioned grounds for impeachment, are relatively straightforward. The Constitution expressly defines "treason,"[13] though, as we shall see, Congress may use a more colloquial or less technical understanding of the term as conspiring or mounting an attack to subvert the government of the United States or state governments. "Bribery" may refer to either the common-law understanding of bribery as using one's office for personal gain or a statutory definition as set forth in the United States Code. And the words "other high" suggest that whatever follows is of the same order of seriousness or magnitude as the terms preceding it (i.e., "treason" and "bribery"). This tells us that not every crime or misdemeanor will count as an impeachable offense but rather that the other high crimes and misdemeanors that are impeachable impose the same degree of harm or threat to the Constitution or to the republic as either trea-son or bribery. Note as well that, whereas treason might entail some official's misconduct to undermine American government or national security, bribery could be a private transaction in which the harm is the corruption of the of-fice itself.

These terms, borrowed from the colonies and British practice, represented technical language that was under-stood during the founding to refer to "political crimes," or abuses power that people in high office might commit by virtue of their positions of power. Yet some modern-day commentators, lawyers, and pundits mistakenly focus on the word "crimes" without considering, as they should, its context. Ripping that term out of context without any ac-knowledgment of the importance of its placement within the constitutional provision is at best lazy constitutional interpretation; as the eminent constitutional scholar Akhil Amar asserts, doing so engages in "blinkered textualism" or "clause-bound" interpretation—trying to read a term (or terms) in the Constitution detached from its context and the rest of the document.[14]

Recourse to the discussions about these terms in the Constitutional Convention and state ratifying conventions, as well as impeachment practices in Congress, should settle any doubts about their meanings. Virtually every example of an impeachable offense mentioned during those conven-tions was made in explicit reference to the president and to an abuse of power by the president that was not redress-able via any other type of legal proceeding. The framers and ratifiers spoke, for example, of impeachable misconduct as "neglect of duty," "misconduct in office," "corrupt administration," "attempts to subvert the Constitution," and various abuses of power including using their powers to shield people with whom they were in criminal concert or to benefit foreign interests at the expense of the United States.[15] James Wilson, delegate to the Pennsylvania ratifying convention and later appointed by President Washington to the Supreme Court, explained shortly after ratification that impeachment was reserved to "political crimes and misdemeanors." He explained that impeachable offenses do not come within "the sphere of ordinary jurisprudence. They are founded on different principles; are governed by different maxims; and are directed to different objects."[16] During the North Carolina ratifying convention, another future Supreme Court justice, James Iredell, explained that impeachment was "calculated to bring [offenders] to punishment for crime which is not easy to describe, but which everyone must be convinced is a high crime and misdemeanor against government. The occasion for its exercise will arise from acts of great injury to the community." Iredell thought that presidents would be impeachable for "receiving a bribe or act[ing] from some corrupt motive or other," not merely for "want of judgment."[17] In *The Federalist Papers*, Hamilton characterized impeachable offenses as arising from "the misconduct of public men, or in other words from the abuse or violation of some public trust." Such offenses were, in his judgment, "[p]olitical, as they relate chiefly to injuries done immediately to the society itself."[18] Interestingly, as the next section shows, the framers' choice of Congress, particularly the Senate as the venue for impeachment trials, turned on their common understanding of what the impeachment process entailed.

III

A common misconception about impeachment is that it is a political proceeding. It derives from the assumption that, because Congress wields the impeachment authority, its proceedings must therefore be political and thus prone to the problems we commonly associate with elected legislatures, especially hyper-partisanship.

Yet this misconception of impeachment obscures (and indeed ignores) why the framers vested the impeachment authority in the two chambers of Congress. The framers did not expect or even want impeachment to be political in its most negative aspects as pure or nasty partisanship. So why did they choose Congress to wield this authority, especially in cases involving presidential misconduct?

One reason is that the framers wished to place the impeachment authority beyond the control of the president and other officials who may become subjected to it. This meant that the framers had to choose between one of the other branches or else establish a special institution such as a privy council. The Article III judiciary did not make sense, since the president might have appointed the judges who would be charged with considering his possible impeachment and removal. The executive branch was out of the question so as to avoid the absurdity of having a president answer only to himself or subject to review by people he had appointed.

Thus the framers settled on Congress. The first reason was that Congress itself is a separate branch and independent from the control of any of the persons who might be considered for impeachment. In addition, members of the House are the only part of the federal government chosen directly by the people unlike presidents (who are chosen by the Electoral College) and senators (chosen by state legislatures in the original Constitution). Since presidential and other kinds of misconduct could often be committed against the people or at their expense, the House was thus given the power to vote on articles of impeachment, thereby providing ordinary citizens the means to protect the country from presidential or other kinds of tyranny. Moreover, representatives are politically accountable to the public for their decisions, so voters could hold them responsible for their impeachment decisions. If the public approved of members' actions against a president, they could express it by reelecting them. But if the public disapproved, voters could punish House members for actions taken against a president.

In *Federalist* no. 65, Alexander Hamilton posed and answered an important question: "Where else than in the Senate could have been found a tribunal sufficiently dignified, or sufficiently independent? What other body would likely to feel confidence enough in its own situation, to preserve, unawed and uninfluenced, the necessary impartiality between an individual accused, and the representatives of the people, the accusers?" Hamilton explained:

> The necessity of a numerous court for the trial of impeachments is equally dictated by the nature of the proceeding. This can never be tied down by such strict rules, either in the delineation of the offence by the prosecutors, or in the construction of it by the Judges, as in common cases serve to limit the discretion of courts in favor of personal security. There will be no jury to stand between the Judges, who are to pronounce the sentence of law and the party who is to receive or suffer it. The awful discretion, which a court of impeachment must necessarily have, to doom to honor to infamy the most confidential and the most distinguished characters of the community, forbids the commitment of the trust to a small number of persons.[19]

The framers believed that senators were best suited to meet the challenges of presidential impeachment trials because they were indirectly elected (by their respective state legislatures until the Seventeenth Amendment provided for the direct election of senators), served for terms of six years, and were likely to be people of sufficient learning and stature to rise to the occasion of a presidential impeachment trial to make decisions in the best interests of the nation, the Constitution, and the public.

In 1833, Justice Joseph Story, in a series of commentaries on the Constitution, reaffirmed and explained in greater detail why Congress, especially the Senate, was the most sensible choice as a court of impeachment. Most important, he noted that the "offences to which the power of impeachment has been, and is ordinarily applied, as a remedy, are of a political character."[20] He explained further:

Not but that crimes of a strictly legal character fall within the scope of the power . . . but that it has a more enlarged operation, and reaches, what are aptly termed, political offences, growing out of personal misconduct, or gross neglect, or usurpation, or habitual disregard of the public interests, in the discharge of duties of political office. These are so various in their character, and so indefinable in their actual involutions, that it is almost impossible to provide systematically for them by positive law. They must be examined upon very broad and comprehensive principles of public policy and duty. They must be judged by the habits, and rules, and principles of diplomacy, of departmental operations and arrangements, of parliamentary practice, or executive customs and negotiations, of foreign, as well as domestic movements; and in short, by a great variety of circumstances, as well as those, which aggravate, as those, which extenuate, or justify the offensive acts, which do not belong to the judicial character in the ordinary administration of justice, and are far removed from the reach of municipal jurisprudence. . . . They are duties, which are easily understood by statesmen, and are rarely known to judges. A tribunal, composed of the former, would therefore be more competent, in point of intelligence and ability, than the latter, for the discharge of functions.[21]

Put differently, Justice Story's point was that members of Congress, especially senators, would be better informed and qualified than judges to make judgment calls about the duties of public officials and the extent to which their breaches may justify impeachment, removal, and disqualification. Their expertise is making policy, and thus legislators are better suited than judges to make policy-like decisions in sanctioning, or not sanctioning, a president for breaching his duties. In other words, legislators are more expert than judges at rendering judgments that are tantamount to policies regarding the scope of breaches of presidential duties. Especially without a code of impeachable offenses, whether or not something is an impeachable offense is a question of line-drawing by the legislature, a function similar to the exercise of its other powers. The "functions" of governmental officials, according to Story, were better "understood[] and more liberally and justly expounded by statesmen, than by mere lawyers."[22]

Echoing arguments made by Hamilton in *The Federalist Papers*, Justice Story stressed how the context for impeachments is alien to the work of federal judges:

Many of the offences, which will be charged against public men, will be generated by the heats and animosities of party; and the very circumstances, that judges should be called to sit, as umpires, in the controversies of party, would inevitably involve them in the common odium of parti[s]ans, and place them in public opinion, if not, at least in form, in the array on one side, or the other. The habits, too, arising from such functions, will lead them to take a more ardent part in public discussions, and in the vindication of their own political decisions, that seems desirable for those, who are daily called upon to decide the private rights of and claims of men, distinguished for their political consequence, zeal, or activity in the ranks of party. In a free government, like ours, there is a peculiar propriety in withdrawing, as much as possible, all judicial functionaries from the contests of party strife.[23]

The framers chose Congress, rather than courts, to render impeachment decisions because they are driven by, or intertwined with, partisan and political concerns that are the regular business of legislators, not judges. Legislators are thus more adept at managing or balancing the partisan milieu and political machinations to determine whether abuses of power actually occurred.

Yet neither chamber (House or Senate) is free to do anything it feels like. In the federal impeachment process, members of Congress are constrained as to the scope of and grounds for decision-making. The Constitution, which declares itself the "supreme law of the land,"[24] circumscribes congressional judgments about various matters within the process, including its grounds, procedures, and sanctions. Impeachment proceedings are unique because they arise at the intersection of politics and constitutional law or, as Charles Black suggested in his seminal treatise on the subject,[25] are best understood as hybrid events in which political actors are constrained to make certain constitutional decisions. While members of Congress will be aware of and sensitive to partisan forces in their decision-making, they are by design politically accountable for their decisions and required to abide by the various safeguards unique to the impeachment process, including the two-thirds threshold for convictions by the Senate. (Those safeguards are not present in the usual lawmaking decisions in Congress, except for the requirement of at least two-thirds of each chamber to override presidential vetoes.)

Nevertheless, the 1913 ratification of the Seventeenth Amendment, which vested the selection of senators in the people rather than in state legislatures, likely has increased the likelihood of partisan concerns impeding convictions and removals. I say "impeding" because convictions require at least two-thirds approval of the Senate, which is a difficult threshold to meet, especially to oust a president. The unlikelihood of one party controlling more than two-thirds of the Senate makes it correspondingly unlikely that either party has enough members to push through a conviction for purely partisan reasons. In short, the process is designed to make conviction and removal difficult. This design also means that obstructing conviction and removal is easier given that all it requires is for at least one-third of the Senate to refuse to convict for partisan reasons. This dynamic is borne out by our history of presidential impeachments, none of which has resulted in a conviction and removal from office.

While James Madison initially objected to having the Senate function as the court of impeachment because it made presidents "improperly dependent" on the Senate for "any act which might be called a [misdemeanor]," [26] the delegates eventually agreed that, between the Senate and the courts, the Senate's size and political accountability made the Senate the more appropriate venue for trying presidential impeachments.

IV

Another feature of the federal impeachment process that can be confusing is the framers' choice of the Chief Justice of the United States to preside over presidential impeachment trials. In other impeachment trials, the vice president usually presides (since the Constitution names the vice president as Presiding Officer of the Senate), though Senate rules allow the Senate Pro Tempore (the longest-serving member of the majority party) to preside in case the vice president is unavailable. It is easy to see why the framers did not want the vice president to preside over presidential impeachment trials, since vice presidents would benefit—by ascending to the presidency—from the conviction and removal of the incumbent president.

But since the framers chose the Senate rather than judges to sit as the court in presidential impeachment trials because the president might have nominated them, the same concern could arise with the Chief Justice, who is, of course, a presidential appointee. The possibility that the president appointed the presiding officer for his own impeachment trial has led generations of Americans to wonder whether that was an oversight in framing the Constitution, along with other perennial concerns such as whether, in presiding, the

Chief Justice wielded the same powers as a trial judge in regular courts.

The framers, of course, could have chosen someone other than the Chief Justice to avoid the problem of having a presiding officer who had a conflict of interest with the president. After all, the Chief Justice might have a conflict of interest aside from the fact that the Chief Justice might owe his job to the president. Chief Justices might have many other conflicts of interest with presidents. There might be personal enmity between the two. Chief Justice John Marshall and President Jefferson, for example, had bad blood between them well before they each took office. The Chief Justice might harbor political ambitions. For instance, Chief Justice Salmon Chase's own presidential ambitions led him to make self-serving decisions throughout the impeachment trial of President Andrew Johnson. There might be sharp, irreconcilable ideological differences between the two. For example, President Franklin Roosevelt repeatedly bashed Chief Justice Charles Evans Hughes and the Supreme Court for blocking key elements of his New Deal. Any of these could possibly lead a Chief Justice (whose own appointment as Chief Justice was the result of a political decision by some president) to be less than perfectly neutral during a presidential impeachment trial. The framers likely foresaw many of these difficulties, but they chose the Chief Justice anyway, a decision that is still problematic given that, as Justice Story noted, having jurists becoming enmeshed in the political firestorm of an impeachment trial is at odds with their constitutional functions, temperaments, and duties.

Yet the choice of the Chief Justice still might make sense for two reasons. The first is that, particularly at the time of the founding, vice presidents were not genuine partners with the presidents whom they served under; the vice president was merely the candidate who had finished second in the race for the presidency. Thus, vice presidents would have been the political rivals of the presidents whose impeachment trials they would have overseen had they been given that power. As originally designed, impeachments literally overturned the results of a presidential election by replacing an ousted president with his principal opponent.

The Twelfth Amendment fixed this problem by ensuring that vice presidents were chosen by the president.[27] While it is true vice presidents could harbor political ambitions after the ratification of the Twelfth Amendment, the ensuing conflict of interest they may have with presidents could be the opposite of the concerns of the framers; now vice presidents might have vested interests in saving presidents from conviction and removal. They could, in other words, benefit either way in a trial: a conviction would make them president, but an acquittal could endear them to the president's party and clear a path to the presidency. Either way there is a conflict, and barring the vice president from presiding over presidential impeachment trials still makes sense.

The second reason is practical: the framers knew that the number of people eligible to serve as presiding officers over presidential impeachment trials was not only small but also likely to be composed of people who knew and were friends with, or foes of, the president. Members of Congress, justices, cabinet officers, and any other high-ranking officials would probably know each other and have personal histories. Of all these people, the one official who might have the best chance to rise above petty personal or partisan concerns was the Chief Justice, who had a vested interest in maintaining the integrity of the Court itself.

In his commentaries on the federal impeachment process, Justice Story, who came to the Court as one of the nation's preeminent legal scholars, recognized the force of this second justification for having the Chief Justice preside over presidential impeachment trials. He recognized "the necessity of excluding the vice president from the chair, when he might have a manifest interest, which would destroy his impartiality," but he also added that "one of the circumstances, most important in the discharge of judicial duties, [is] that they rarely carry with them any strong popular favour, or popular influence. The influence, if any, is of a different sort, arising from dignity of life and conduct, abstinence from political contests, exclusive devotion to the advancement of the law, and a firm administration of justice; circumstances, which are felt more by the profession, than they can be expected to be praised by the public."[28] Precisely because presidential impeachment trials are political firestorms, the Chief Justice is a better choice than any other possible candidates to preside since he or she is insulated from direct public or partisan pressures and immune to political retaliation. Whether this circumstance is empirically true in any given trial is a different question than why the Constitution mandates that the Chief Justice preside over presidential impeachment trials.

Given that the Constitution requires the Chief Justice to preside over presidential impeachment trials, there remains a question: What kinds of powers may they wield in such proceedings? Trial judges wield considerable authority in running their courtrooms, including ruling on questions of evidence and procedure. But is the Chief Justice supposed to have the same range of powers when presiding over presidential impeachment trials?

The answer is almost certainly "no." The framers did not design impeachment proceedings as legal proceedings; the ultimate decision makers are senators rather than laypeople or judges, the sanctions are limited to removal and disqualification and are not the kinds available in civil or criminal proceedings, the grounds for conviction and removal are primarily political in nature (entailing the kinds of abuses of power that may arise only from people in power), and the rules governing the entire process derive from the most important political document in America, the Constitution. Indeed, the rules of the Senate (deriving legitimacy from Article I, section 5) governing impeachment trials delineate the relationship between the Chief Justice and senators, the most important element of which is that any ruling by the Chief Justice is appealable to the Senate as a whole, which may overrule him by majority vote. Any other scenario in which the Chief Justice could make rulings that either are not appealable to the Senate or any other entity or are appealable to the Court itself makes no sense, since any other arrangement would be vesting the ultimate power over impeachments or removals outside of Congress and therefore would be impossible to square with the constitutional directive that the House has the "sole power to impeach" and the Senate has "the sole power to try all impeachments."

V

In American history, the House of Representatives has impeached 20 people, 14 being lower court judges. Of the 20 different people whom the House has impeached, the Senate has convicted and removed only eight officials, all of them lower court judges. Because all judges, including Supreme Court justices, have different functions and tenures than presidents, a persistent concern has been whether the standards and timing for impeachments should be different for judges than for president.

All Article III judges serve "during good behavior," which has been accepted to mean life tenure unless they do something egregiously wrong, in which case they may be impeached by the House, convicted by the Senate, and removed from office.[29] For offenses falling short of impeachable misconduct, federal judges are still subject to sanctions so long as the sanction is not tantamount to the punishments uniquely available through the impeachment process (i.e., removal and disqualification). Indeed, four federal trial judges (Harry Claiborne, Walter Nixon, Alcee Hastings, and Thomas Porteous) were criminally prosecuted before they were impeached by the House; two of them (Claiborne and Nixon) were convicted and imprisoned before any impeachment proceedings in the House began. Hastings and Claiborne each challenged their prosecutions in court, claiming that as federal judges they were entitled to immunity from criminal prosecution unless or until they were impeached and removed from office. Two appellate courts rejected this argument. In the Hastings matter, a panel of three judges on the United States Court of Appeals for the District of Columbia explained:

> We are not persuaded that the proposed rule of absolute judicial immunity from criminal prosecution is a necessary compliment to the Constitution's explicit protections [of life tenure and undiminished compensation]. Indeed, the miniscule increment in judicial independence that might be derived from the proposed rule would be outweighed by the tremendous harm that the rule would cause to another treasured value of our constitutional system: no man in this country is so high that he is above the law. . . . A judge no less than any other man is subject to the processes of the criminal law.[30]

Claiborne challenged his prosecution on the grounds that as a federal judge he was entitled to immunity from any criminal prosecution until he had been impeached and removed from office or left his judgeship voluntarily. A special panel from the Ninth Circuit federal court of appeals agreed with the *United States v. Hastings* decision[31] and the earlier decision of a federal appellate court that reached the same conclusion in *United States v. Isaacs*.[32] "No man in this country is so high that he is above the law. No officer of the law may set that law at defiance with impunity. All the officers of the government, from the highest to the lowest, are creatures of the law, and bound to obey it. It is only the supreme power in our system of government, and every man who by accepting office participates in its functions is only the more strongly bound to submit to that supremacy, and to observe the limitations which it imposes upon the exercise of the authority which it gives."[33] In addition, the Court reasoned that "it [was] unlikely that judicial independence would be measurably diminished by subjecting judges to the processes of the criminal laws."[34] The special panel noted a number of procedural protections against abusive prosecutions that would apply with equal if not greater force in cases of criminal prosecutions of sitting federal judges. After citing the reasoning in the *Hastings* decision, the *Claiborne* court concluded: "It can scarcely be doubted that the citizenry would justifiably lose respect for and confidence in a system of government under which judges were apparently held to be above the processes of criminal law."[35]

However, some scholars contend that presidents should not be treated the same as lower court judges for impeachment purposes. First, they have different kinds of tenure. Judges serve for life, while presidents do not. Since federal judges are not subject to elections or reelections once they assume office, the only practical and legitimate way to sanction them is through either criminal prosecutions or impeachment. But since presidents are elected, so the argument goes, they could be removed by means other than impeachment, namely, by being defeated for reelection or, as Richard Nixon did, resigning from office. Therefore, presidents unlike judges can be expected to rotate out of office in time to be prosecuted later. The argument goes further that, because of the president's unique position as the singular head of the entire executive branch of government, criminal prosecutions could seriously interfere with its functioning. Prosecuting judges (or even justices) does not have the potential to paralyze the entire federal judiciary, whereas prosecuting presidents could so distract them that the executive branch could be disrupted and paralyzed while a president endures criminal prosecution or conviction. This argument has especially strong appeal among the public and commentators because they are invested in presidents in ways that they are not invested in Article III judges or justices; they want the executive to fulfill the duties of the office without being distracted by (potentially) partisan prosecutions.

The argument can go further to suggest that the grounds for impeaching presidents should be different than those for lower court judges. The eight judges who were convicted in their Senate trials were removed for such misconduct as lying under oath and engaging in misconduct that damaged the integrity of the office. Their misconduct effectively disabled them from doing their jobs because integrity is integral to what they do. In contrast, presidents are not necessarily disabled by similar misconduct, because integrity may not be as integral for them to do their jobs as it is for judges and justices. Moreover, voters can ratify their misconduct, as (they arguably did) with the election of Donald Trump in 2016 and the reelection of Bill Clinton in 1996. Americans were not distressed by concerns that these or other presidents somehow lacked moral integrity, because they could still deliver on what they had pledged to do as presidents.

These considerations do not, however, require presidents to be treated differently for impeachment purposes. They may persuade members of Congress to treat them differently, but members could be persuaded that a president's moral failings are too substantial to ignore their degradation of the office. Because impeachment authority is vested in members of Congress, who are politically accountable, they may consider the possible ratification of presidents' misconduct by the American people. They may consider whether the costs of removal are outweighed by whatever good the president is doing in office. At the same time, members may decide that the costs of keeping presidents in office are too high, as they may damage the rule of law or the importance (in the views of some members) of a president's moral character to his office.

Moreover, the Supreme Court's 2020 decision in *Trump v. Vance* did for presidents what the two appellate court decisions had done for federal judges and is consistent with how those courts resolved the question of whether federal judges are entitled to special immunity from criminal prosecutions. In *Trump v. Vance*,[36] the Court, voting 7 to 2, rejected the same argument made on behalf of then–President Trump, who was resisting complying with a subpoena from the local district attorney in Manhattan. Indeed, in the *Claiborne*, *Hastings*, and *Trump* cases, lawyers seized on the argument that the Constitution's provision that "the party convicted [in an impeachment trial] shall nevertheless be liable and subject to indictment, trial, judgment, and punishment, according to the law,"[37] suggested that prosecutions must follow rather than be allowed to precede impeachments. However, the appellate courts read the language as indicating that criminal prosecutions and impeachments are independent from each other, and thus the Constitution does not require that one must precede the other or even be a required precondition for the other.

To be sure, the immediate question in *Trump v. Vance* had to do with whether sitting presidents were immune from having to comply with judicial subpoenas in criminal proceedings. The Court initially rejected the possibility of "distraction" from performing his constitutional duties entitled the president to such immunity. The Court explained that "two centuries of experience confirm that a properly tailored criminal subpoena will not normally hamper the performance of the President's constitutional duties." Then, following the Court's reasoning in *Clinton v. Jones* that sitting presidents are not immune from damage actions based on misconduct prior to taking office, the Court in *Trump v. Vance* "found that the risk of [political] harassment was not 'serious' because federal courts have the tools to defer and, where necessary, dismiss vexatious civil suits. And, while we cannot ignore that state prosecutors may have political motivations, here again the law seeks to protects against the predicted abuse." The Court emphasized that "safeguards" such as restrictions on grand juries and fishing expeditions protect presidents (as they protect all citizens) from improperly motivated prosecutions.[38]

Context matters. Indeed, it is the most important thing. Judges and presidents have different duties, of course. Judges have the duty to decide cases or controversies as laid out in Article III of the Constitution; Article II charges presidents "to take care to execute the laws faithfully." But that does not mean they should be treated differently as a matter of constitutional law in their respective impeachment proceedings. It just means that the contexts or circumstances in which their abuses of power may arise are different: They can abuse their respective powers differently and with possibly different ramifications. But while they are subject to different kinds of accountability, impeachment is among them for both. The differences turn on the different contexts in which abuses and the need for removal and disqualification might arise.

Yet some members of Congress could believe in good faith that Bill Clinton's lying and perjury (as determined by a federal judge after he left office) were not so important as to require conviction and removal, given that the American people knew or accepted the fact that he was a moral degenerate and still voted for him anyway. The same could be said of Trump: that he proved to be, in office, the con man that people knew before they voted for him did not change the value some members of Congress believed his presidency had. And of course, voters could change their minds, as they arguably did when they did not reelect Trump. With Trump running for a third time for the presidency in 2024, his moral shortcomings will again be on the ballot.

The public's ratification of presidential misconduct is not, however, a constitutional directive obviating impeachment. Impeachment was designed as a separate mechanism for holding presidents accountable for misconduct in office. Members of Congress could take popular ratification into account when making decisions regarding presidential impeachments, but the Constitution does not require them to do so. In other words, impeachment allows Congress to render a separate judgment from that of the voting public on the propriety of allowing a president who has committed serious misconduct to remain in office.

Moreover, members of Congress are not required by the Constitution to conclude that, because federal judges may be convicted, removed, and even disqualified for lying under oath or bribery, presidents must be, too. The relative gravity and ramifications of these various officials' actions could be different, and members of Congress are entitled to take into account the full context in which misconduct arises when determining the propriety of convicting and removing presidents from office. Accordingly, Congress decided that Judge Claiborne's income tax fraud robbed him of the moral authority to continue to sit in judgment of other people convicted of the same wrongdoing, but members of Congress could decide that presidents guilty of the same misconduct might still have sufficient moral authority to continue to do their jobs. Members of Congress could decide otherwise, too, if they are persuaded that the fraud was so extensive, or so intertwined with the moral authority presidents need to oversee the administration of the system of criminally prosecuting people for income tax fraud, that they should no longer be allowed to remain office. In either event, the decision makers themselves are accountable for their judgments.

VI

There are several recurring procedural questions in impeachment history, especially in presidential impeachment trials. The first is whether the Due Process Clause of the Fifth Amendment applies to impeachment proceedings. If it does, the House and the Senate each then might have to guarantee certain procedural safeguards beyond those specified in the Constitution for officials who are the subjects of impeachment proceedings.

There are, however, two reasons why concerns about the possible applicability of the Due Process Clause to impeachment proceedings are misplaced. The first is that its minimal requirements are easily satisfied and have been in every impeachment in history. These requirements are (1) neutral or impartial decision-making and (2) notice. The House and the Senate are the Constitution's designated authorities in impeachment proceedings. Whatever issues people have had with these authorities' impartiality in such proceedings, the Constitution answers them by vesting "sole" authority in each chamber to conduct such proceedings. Notice is easily provided in impeachment hearings; by impeaching a president, the House has given ample notice of the charges against him.

Second, the law of due process does not apply to impeachment proceedings. Due process is a concern if a protected interest in property, liberty, or life is on the brink of being deprived by the government. The liberty interest protected by procedural due process is the freedom to move one's body about. Since the sanctions in an impeachment trial do not include any of those available in criminal proceedings, such as imprisonment, there is no liberty interest at stake in an impeachment trial. The life interest protected by due process is the freedom to live or to be alive. Given that removal and disqualification are the only sanctions available in impeachment trials, there is no protected life interest at stake in a Senate impeachment trial. And the property interest protected by due process turns on whether the law gives rise to a reasonable expectation of some entitlement of ownership. A president does not have a protected property interest in his job because he takes the job on the condition that he does not commit an impeachable offense.

Nevertheless, the framers took great pains to provide safeguards to protect against abuse of the impeachment power, safeguards that were not available to the people of England or the American colonists. For all impeachable officials, including judges and presidents, these safeguards included dividing the power between the two chambers of Congress; vesting the final authority of removal in the Senate (whose members were thought to be more capable than their House counterparts of rising above petty partisan politics for the sake of the country and the Constitution); and requiring that at least two-thirds of the Senate approve conviction and removal from office. For presidents, the Constitution provides further safeguards by requiring that the Chief Justice preside and that senators be on oath or affirmation.

It is noteworthy that Senate impeachment trials have accorded presidents (and other impeached officials) plenty of protections, including the opportunity to cross-examine witnesses, to present their defenses, to introduce evidence, to rebut arguments or presentations made by House impeachment Managers (members of the House appointed to prosecute the case for conviction in the Senate), and to conduct discovery. Furthermore, the modern practice in presidential impeachment trials has been for the Senate majority and minority leaders to negotiate a mutually agreed arrangement to fill any gaps in the rules. Senator Trent Lott, who was the Senate Majority Leader, and Senator Tom Daschle, who was the Minority Leader, worked out a detailed arrangement to govern President Bill Clinton's trial. Twenty years later, Majority Leader Mitch McConnell and Minority Leader Chuck Schumer agreed on a sketchier arrangement for Donald Trump's first Senate impeachment trial. Though Trump was no longer president during his second trial, Schumer and McConnell had swapped leadership positions but agreed on the arrangements for the second trial. These protections exceeded the minimal safeguards that due process requires.

The next recurring procedural question is whether the Constitution requires or imposes on impeachment proceedings specific rules of evidence or burdens of proof. The silence of the Constitution and the Senate rules on these subjects is not important for two reasons.

The first is the longstanding recognition within the Senate that no uniform burdens of proof or evidentiary rules are enforceable against individual senators. As a practical matter, it is impossible to prove that a senator has not applied the "proper" or "required" burden of proof or evidentiary rules. Enforcing uniform burdens or rules requires getting into the minds of senators, and that is of course impossible. If senators swear that they are following the rules, then there is no way to prove otherwise. Because the Senate as an institution has recognized this for years, the Senate allows each senator to adopt whichever burden of proof and whichever evidentiary rules he or she deems appropriate.

Second, burdens of proof and evidentiary rules are designed to guide or help lay jurors navigate through legal proceedings. They are safeguards to provide guidance to lay jurors, who are not trained in the law, from merely doing whatever they feel like doing, including ignoring the rules, when considering evidence or rendering judgments. A fundamental assumption in vesting senators with the authority to conduct presidential impeachment trials is that senators are more sophisticated than typical lay jurors and thus are able to evaluate the weight and credibility of evidence without the need for rules telling them how to do so. In contrast, for example, the Federal Rules of Evidence places limitations on the use of hearsay in criminal proceedings, that is, information received from other people that cannot be substantiated. Lay jurors are often instructed to ignore hearsay evidence (or not to give it any weight in their deliberations) because they may not appreciate how unreliable it is. Senators, however, are presumed sufficiently experienced to make their own judgments about the weight and credibility of various kinds of evidence. In impeachment trials, they each rely on their own judgment, knowledge, and skills in assessing the evidence presented.

Burdens of proof are handled the same as in impeachment proceedings. In civil trials, the burden of proof that applies is a preponderance of the evidence, meaning that the party with the burden must convince the factfinder that there is a greater than 50% chance that an assertion or claim is valid. In criminal proceedings, the burden of proof is tougher, requiring the party carrying the burden (the government) to persuade the fact finder that assertions or claims made have been established beyond a reasonable doubt. Obviously, this tougher burden makes criminal convictions more difficult.

As a practical matter, the Senate allows each senator to decide individually what burden of proof to apply. The uniqueness of the proceedings—not civil, not criminal—leads many senators to adopt a hybrid burden of proof that is similar to the one used in certain administrative proceedings: the clear and convincing standard. This standard requires that the evidence presented must be highly and substantially more likely to be true than not true. This standard is tougher than the burden of proof in civil proceedings but not as tough as the one employed in criminal proceedings.

VII

In this section, I examine how the different mechanisms for checking presidential misconduct may fit together or be coordinated. Because presidents are distinct from other officials in their being more visible and subject to more scrutiny, uniquely situated as the only individual in charge of a single branch of government, and having unique powers such as the bully pulpit, holding them accountable for misconduct may appear chaotic, uncertain, and difficult to navigate. Are presidents subject to conviction and removal for the same offenses as other impeachable officials, such as judges, who are not selected by the same means? If the voters go so far as to ratify presidential misconduct, is that the end of the matter? Is impeachment off the table after that? Occam's razor suggests that with competing theories the preferable course is to adopt the simplest one, and the simplest explanation is that the various mechanisms for holding presidents accountable are not mutually exclusive; each has its own peculiar focus. Each is constitutionally permissible, but none is constitutionally compelled.

For example, elections focus on misconduct prior to being in office and, for incumbents, on performance in office. Thus presidents may argue, as did Bill Clinton in 1998 and Donald Trump more loudly and repeatedly in 2019, that impeachments should not be preferred over—or seek to overturn—elections. Presidents have strong incentives to define the scope of impeachable offenses narrowly and to have elections serve as the venue for nearly or perhaps all the questions that get asked about moral failings or misconduct. An obvious problem with such arguments is that a reelected president, such as Richard Nixon and Bill Clinton, may no longer rely on elections to check their misconduct. Moreover, one important purpose of impeachment is to serve as a check against presidents rigging elections in their favor, including using the powers of the office to go after political enemies. No other mechanism seems nearly as well suited as impeachment to address such types of presidential misconduct.

In 1982, the United States Supreme Court ruled that Richard Nixon was absolutely immune from lawsuits seeking damages for any of his official acts as president. To assuage concerns that its decision might have made it more difficult to ensure presidential accountability for misconduct, the Court, voting 5 to 4, added that there are several other means for doing so: impeachment, media coverage, congressional oversight, elections, popularity, and presidents' concerns about their legacies. The list is not comprehensive, since there are other methods for checking presidential misconduct, such as civil suits for damages based on misconduct prior to taking office (*Clinton v. Jones*), criminal subpoenas (*Trump v. Vance*), and possibly censure.

Censure might be most appropriate for misconduct falling short of impeachable misconduct. When the Constitution declares that "[j]udgment in cases of impeachment shall not extend further than to removal from office[] and disqualification to hold and enjoy any office of honor, trust, or profit under the United States,"[39] it arguably implies that some judgments that fall short of removal and disqualification may be permissible. At the same time, impeachment is not available for all kinds of misconduct. For those offenses falling short of treason, bribery, and other high crimes or misdemeanors, or those not triggering or entailing the use of removal and disqualification, it seems plausible that some mechanism less serious than such sanctions could be used without incurring any constitutional difficulty. Censure could be one such option, particularly if it does not comprise an illegal bill of attainder (a legislative decision imposing punishment on someone in the absence of a judicial trial).

Another theme apparent in the history and practice of impeachment in America is that various mechanisms are not mutually exclusive. For example, while *Clinton v. Jones* upholds the constitutionality of civil actions based on misconduct prior to taking office, it is possible that some such misconduct might be very serious and bear on a president's fitness (and legitimacy) to serve. What if a presidential candidate hid from voters long-standing support for and membership in the Ku Klux Klan? Such a lie might be hard to redress through a civil lawsuit, but it seems well-suited for impeachment, particularly because it has a connection with the office that the president was able to secure by hiding this background. Similarly, the presidential candidate could hide evidence of a pattern of sexual assault or murder. Keeping that information from voters undermines the integrity of the presidential election and therefore has a plausible connection to the president's current position. (Interestingly, one of the grounds on which the House impeached and the Senate convicted, removed, and disqualified one federal judge was his perjury on the Senate questionnaire required to be completed as part of his background check for the federal judgeship to which he had been appointed.[40]) The nexus, along with the gravity of the misconduct, makes such misconduct a legitimate basis for impeachment.

Even if there is no direct nexus between the misconduct and the office, such as a president's chronic philandering or a murder for which he was acquitted, there is still likely a significant negative impact on the president's capacity to serve. Impeachment exists in part as a safeguard for the republic from a president's corruption of the processes by which he achieved office, exercised power, or undertook efforts to stay in office.

The overlap between impeachments and legal processes for holding presidents accountable for misconduct has raised concerns among presidents and others about two other procedural issues. The first is whether res judicata (treating a decision on the merits of a claim as final) or collateral estoppel (treating resolution of an issue in prior proceedings as the final settlement of those questions in other cases) apply in impeachment proceedings. In the late 1980s, Alcee Hastings filed a lawsuit challenging the constitutionality of Judicial Council proceedings referring his misconduct to the House for consideration as a basis for impeachment. The Circuit Court of Appeals for the District of Columbia ruled that Hastings was estopped from raising his constitutional claims in any further proceedings.[41] The House and the Senate did not apply either res judicata or collateral estoppel in the Hastings impeachment proceedings (or the other two judicial impeachments in the late 1980s) based on the different burdens of proof applying in different legal proceedings and the value of allowing impeached officials to introduce evidence not admissible in prior legal proceedings and of allowing senators to decide for themselves which burdens or rules of evidence they would follow.

The second issue has been the extent to which the Constitution's prohibitions against double jeopardy under the Fifth and Fourteenth Amendments precludes impeaching a president for something for which he has already been absolved or acquitted. It plainly does not, since double jeopardy arises only when someone is "subject for the same offense to be twice put in jeopardy of life or limb."[42] Double jeopardy precludes criminal actions brought against someone for the same misconduct twice. Yet in the impeachment process, the sanctions are not criminal; no one is being subject to having their life or liberty curtailed as a result of an impeachment conviction. Thus, when the former judge Harry Claiborne was subjected to impeachment after having been convicted of tax fraud, there was no double jeopardy problem. Similarly, when Alcee Hastings was subjected to impeachment after having been acquitted of bribery and perjury, there was no double jeopardy problem. The answer is no different for a president who faces legal or other liability for the misconduct for which he has faced impeachment. Indeed, the Constitution says that "the party convicted [in an impeachment trial] shall nevertheless be liable and subject to indictment, trial, judgment, and punishment, according to law,"[43] is a clear directive that double jeopardy does not bar an impeached official from facing legal liability for misconduct.

Last but hardly least, the impeachment decisions or practices of Congress are not binding on future Congresses. Future Congresses may reach different judgments, or they may choose to follow what members decided earlier on the matters in question. These practices are precedents, which Congress may choose to follow (or not), just as the Supreme Court may choose to uphold or overrule its prior rulings. For example, the very first Congress impeached William Blount, but the Senate did not convict him due in part to the votes of many senators who thought that the Senate lacked jurisdiction because he had been a senator; their reading of the Constitution was that senators were not subject to impeachment. A future Congress may decide to reject that reading, although none has yet done so.

The fact that the House and Senate each make judgments that are not binding on either chamber in the future leads some people to have less confidence in the system, since it appears more fluid or less rigid than they might have expected it to be. Yet the House and Senate almost always follow their own traditions, just as the Supreme Court usually follows precedents set by prior constitutional decisions. The main differences are that the impeachment process is considerably more transparent than the Court's constitutional decision-making and that members of Congress, but not the justices, are politically accountable for their choices.

The Impeachment and Trial of Andrew Johnson

Andrew Johnson, in office from 1865 to 1869, was the first president to be impeached, but he was not the first to face the threat of impeachment. Serving earlier, from 1829 to 1836, Andrew Jackson was the first president threatened with impeachment. Though Jackson was enormously popular, having won election and reelection by large margins in 1828 and 1832, an entirely new political party—the Whigs— had been formed in opposition to the perceived tyrannies of his presidency, including vigorous use of the veto to strike down federal laws strengthening or expanding the reach of the national government. Jackson championed the common man against rapacious businesses and banks, but Henry Clay, Jackson's nemesis in the Senate, and other members of the opposition Whig Party mocked his presidency as a "mobacracy."

Clay championed the National Bank as an important extension of federal power to safely hold federal deposits, lend government money to people in need, establish a uniform currency, and promote business and industry by extending credit. When, in Jackson's second term, Treasury Secretary William Duane refused to follow his orders to remove all federal deposits from the National Bank and place them in state banks' repositories, Jackson fired him. He replaced

Duane with Roger Taney, the United States Attorney General, who moved the deposits as Jackson had directed. Clay and his fellow Whigs regarded the moves undermining the National Bank as abuses of power. Rather than seek impeachment in the House, which Democrats controlled, Clay took to the floor of the Senate on December 26, 1833, to read a series of resolutions condemning Jackson's dismantling of the National Bank. He condemned Jackson for having usurped congressional power, for destroying a congressionally sanctioned agency, for his illegal discharge of a cabinet officer without the consent of the Senate (which the Tenure in Office Act required), for his abuse of his veto powers, and for his corruption of the civil service with the spoils system, which favored giving loyal political supporters jobs in the administration. A legendary orator, Clay spoke for more than two days, unleashing his rhetorical firepower to condemn Jackson for actions that would eventually cause Congress to "die—ignobly die" and transform its members to "base, mean, adject slaves," who would earn the "scorn and contempt of mankind" and die "unpitied, unwept, unmourned!" When warned by his fellow Whigs that Jackson's followers might try to kill him, Clay responded, "The scoundrels dare not approach me. Their assassination is of characters, not of persons."[1] Deflecting the attacks of Democrats in the Senate, including the vitriol of Vice President Martin Van Buren, Clay pushed the matter to a vote, ultimately persuading the Senate to formally censure Jackson (voting 26–20 in favor) and Taney (28–18). True to form, Jackson stood his ground and filed a formal protest (written by Taney), which the Whig-dominated Senate rejected, 27 to 16.

Jackson acknowledged that a president may be impeached for "high crimes and misdemeanors," be "indicted and punished by law" for his misconduct, be "liable" to any third parties injured by his misconduct, be subject to "criminal prosecution," and be "accountable at the bar of public opinion for every act of his administration." Yet he argued that "only" these were the appropriate mechanisms for holding presidents accountable for their misconduct, and he stressed that censure lacked any express authorization in the Constitution and was "an impeachment" not made through the proper procedures as set forth in the Constitution. Moreover, he noted that none of his actions were impeachable; thus censure was an unconstitutional attempt to bypass impeachment, which, he emphasized, was within the "exclusive" province of the House to initiate. "[I]t is obvious," he said, "that the vague, general, and abstract form of the resolution is in perfect keeping with those other departures from first principles and settled improvements in jurisprudence so properly the boast of free countries in modern times." He then meticulously showed how each of the actions for which he was being censured were legitimate exercises of executive power.[2] When Whigs in the Senate did not relent, he campaigned against them and succeeded in helping to elect a new Democratic majority in the Senate, which expunged the censure in January 1837.

The second president threatened with impeachment was John Tyler. Though he modeled himself on Jackson, Tyler was immensely unpopular, particularly since he had left the Democratic Party to become the running mate of the political journeyman William Henry Harrison, the first Whig to be elected president. When Harrison died within a month of his inauguration, Tyler suddenly became president in 1841. While Democrats' hatred for Tyler as a traitor to their cause intensified after he assumed office, Whigs distrusted him as a former ardent Democrat. When he vetoed a law rechartering the National Bank, Tyler was expelled from the Whig Party. He then became, as he liked to say, a man "without a party."

Despite his protests against condemnation from the House for exercising the veto as Jackson had done and for maintaining unilateral control over his nominations, Tyler was subjected to several impeachment attempts. The first was mounted by Representative John Botts, a Whig from Virginia. In the immediate aftermath of Tyler's veto of June 29, 1842, which had followed earlier vetoes of other Whig-backed legislation, Botts introduced a resolution to appoint a special committee to investigate whether Tyler had committed an impeachable offense. It was the first resolution ever approved by the House to initiate an impeachment inquiry. When Tyler issued another veto on August 9, 1842, the House referred his formal protest (tracking much of President Jackson's earlier arguments against censure) to a special committee that included Botts as a member and a former president, John Quincy Adams, as its chair.

A week later, the committee issued a scathing report, condemning Tyler's vetoes of two bills attempting to recharter the National Bank for "gross abuse of congressional power and bold assumptions of powers never vested in him by any law"; for having "deprived the people of self-government"; for having "assumed [the] whole Legislative power to himself [and] levying millions of money upon the people, without any authority of law"; and for his "abusive exercise of the constitutional power of the President to arrest the actions of Congress upon measures vital to the welfare of the people." The report then shifted to acknowledge that Tyler's actions might not have been impeachable, because "in the present state of public affairs, [it would] prove abortive." Some House members dissented to the report on the ground that the veto was a unilateral power of the presidency not subject to second-guessing by Congress. After virtually no discussion, the House approved and adopted the report by a vote of 100 to 80. The vote marked the first time that the House of Representatives had censured (i.e., approved a resolution condemning) a president.[3]

Nearly two weeks later, Tyler delivered his formal protest to this latest censure. He underscored the unprecedented nature of the House's referral of his veto to a special committee and the committee's actions in charging him with impeachable offenses but not actually impeaching him. Echoing President Jackson's earlier protest against his censure by the Senate, Tyler argued that, if the charges could not be proved, then the House, which has "the sole power of impeachment," had no discretion to do anything but impeach him—or not. If he were impeached, Tyler said, he at least would have had a chance to defend himself in the Senate, but the House had instead "charged him with violating pledges [to sign Whig-backed bills] which I never gave, [with] usurping powers not conferred upon by the President by law, and, above all, with usurping powers conferred by the Constitution from corrupt motives and for unwarranted ends."[4] Tyler remained steadfastly defiant, maintaining that, if some members of Congress did not approve of his vetoes, then they could amend the Constitution to alter executive prerogative.

Botts persuaded the House to censure Tyler just as the Whigs had censured Jackson. On his motion, the House refused to publish Tyler's protest, just as the Senate had refused to publish Jackson's protest. The House then adopted a resolution that Botts had proposed, which was modeled on the resolution approved by the Senate against Jackson in 1834. The irony was not lost on Tyler or Secretary of State Daniel Webster, who had both voted in favor of that resolution. In the meantime, Botts lost his seat in the House in the midterm elections, and Democrats took control of the House. Botts kept pressing, however, to have the House vote on his resolution, containing nine impeachment articles that he drafted against Tyler. The next day, the House rejected the impeachment resolution by a vote of 127 to 83, marking the first-ever vote in the House on any impeachment resolution. While threats of impeachment persisted against Tyler, none came close to requiring a vote on the House floor.

Four years later, the House voted on a different resolution, this one initially proposed by a new member from the state of Illinois, Abraham Lincoln. On May 13, 1846, President James Polk secured a declaration of war from Congress based on his claim that Mexico had fired the first shots, eventually leading to the Mexican–American War. As his first piece of business when he became a congressman, Lincoln urged the House to approve several resolutions to demand that Polk show the exact "spot" of "soil" where "the blood of our citizens had been spilled."[5] While the House rejected Lincoln's resolutions, it immediately considered a resolution condemning Polk for having begun a war against Mexico "unnecessarily and unconstitutionally," which the House barely approved (82–81), with Lincoln casting the pivotal vote.[6]

Years later, there would be rumblings about impeaching Lincoln during his first years as president because Union forces failed to bring the Civil War to a swift resolution. But it was not until after his assassination that forces came together to impeach, for the first time, an American president. That impeachment and subsequent trial became one of the most significant constitutional events in the country's history.

I

It is hard to overstate how unpopular Andrew Johnson was. A Democrat, he alienated his own party by agreeing to remain in Congress rather than bolt, as other Democrats did, when the Civil War began. When he showed up drunk to the inauguration on March 4, 1865 (the president's and his own), Lincoln demanded that he be taken away and that he not be allowed back in Lincoln's presence. Lincoln ignored Johnson after that.

Yet when Johnson became president after Lincoln's assassination, he made it known that he did not see his duty as merely serving out the remainder of Lincoln's term. Instead, as president, Johnson became an unrepentant Democrat who tried using every power he had to block Reconstruction under the Radical Republicans. He issued 29 vetoes, with Congress overriding 15 of them, the highest percentage yet in American history. Johnson pardoned Confederates, removed Republicans from office, and stripped Union military leaders of command when they did not do as he asked. He repeatedly lambasted Congress profanely and tried (unsuccessfully) to recruit the wildly popular Civil War general Ulysses S. Grant to join his cabinet. (The move was motivated by the desires to preempt Grant from mounting a presidential campaign and to have some of Grant's popularity rub off on Johnson.) While Grant deflected and delayed in responding to Johnson's entreaties, Johnson increasingly intensified his efforts to remove Secretary of War Edwin Stanton, who would not sanction many of his directives for departments and commanders in the field. Johnson consulted with several people, including Attorney General Henry Stanbery and Secretary of the Interior Orville Browning, on how he could rid himself of Stanton. He finally decided the best course of action was to suspend rather than terminate Stanton, which he believed allowed him to avoid the mandate of the Tenure in Office Act, under which removal of a cabinet member required Senate approval beforehand. As he had done three times previously, Johnson had vetoed that Act, but Congress, as it had the previous vetoes, had overridden that veto as well.

Although the House Judiciary Committee previously opposed recommending impeachment by a 5 to 4 vote in July, it reversed course in November. All five members of the majority later approving a report recommending impeachment were Republicans, while two other Republican members of the House joined two Democrats to dissent to the committee's report, which was then forwarded to the entire House for deliberation. In December 1867, the House voted 108 to 57 to adopt the report. Two months later, on February 24, 1868, the House, voting 126 to 47, formally approved an impeachment resolution against Johnson. With that die having been cast, Johnson quickly sent a note to Stanton informing him that he was removed from his post as secretary of the War Department.

While Thaddeus Stevens of Pennsylvania and John Bingham of Ohio were sent to notify the Senate of the House's judgment, the House's work was not yet done. It delegated to the House Judiciary Committee the task of drafting impeachment articles. It approved ten but eventually dropped one as unnecessary and weak. The major focus of the articles that were approved was Johnson's violation of the Tenure in Office Act, which provided that cabinet officials "should hold their offices . . . during the term of the President by whom they may have been appointed, and for one month thereafter, subject to the removal by and with the advice and consent of the Senate."

The charges of violating the Tenure in Office Act made some sense, as it was a duly enacted law of Congress. It was the president's job to "take care to execute the laws faithfully," including the Tenure in Office Act, not to flout the law or undermine it as Johnson had. Because section 5 of the Act provided that anyone who accepted an appointment in violation of the Act was guilty of a high misdemeanor, and section 6 provided that any "removal" or other actions in violation of the Act were defined as high misdemeanors, any statutory violations were grounds for impeachment as well as criminal fines. Besides Johnson's being charged in his impeachment with violating section 6, Lorenzo Thomas, named to replace Stanton, was implicitly charged with violating section 5.

A Radical Republican, Stevens was less than impressed with the substance of these articles. He scolded the House Judiciary Committee for "making a mere pretense of prosecuting impeachment" by citing "the most trifling crimes and misdemeanors." Mostly through intermediaries (he was too weak to speak loudly or walk around the chamber), Stevens said that impeachment was fundamentally about respect for the rule of law. "The Senate had confirmed the Tenure in Office Act. What right had the President to deny, defy, or seek to disobey that law?"[7] Stevens told anyone who would listen that the charges had to involve abuses of power, and he believed Johnson had committed plenty of them. As the House debated Johnson's breaches of the Tenure in Office Act, the passions of House Republicans boiled over. Johnson tried to stem the tide of the growing outrage by dropping his efforts to get the matter before the Supreme Court. His fate was thus left solely in the hands of the House.

House Speaker Schuyler Colfax announced the appointment of seven House members as the impeachment Managers who would prosecute the case in the Senate, including John Bingham of Ohio (who took a leading role in arguing for the Fourteenth Amendment), Benjamin Butler of Massachusetts (who would become lead prosecutor for the House in Johnson's trial), and George Boutwell of Massachusetts (a Radical Republican who helped to draft the Fourteenth Amendment and later became Grant's Treasury secretary). Shortly thereafter, the Managers forwarded two more impeachment articles for approval by the House. The House approved the tenth article, which had been drafted by Butler. It charged Johnson with having "brought the high Office of the President of the United States into contempt, ridicule, and disgrace, to the great scandal of all citizens" by delivering a stump speech in New Orleans promising to "veto [Radical Republicans'] measures whenever any of them come to me." Butler had pushed for the tenth article to counter the idea that only indictable crimes could be impeachable offenses. Working with the moderate James Wilson of Iowa, Stevens delivered the eleventh article, which was a catch-all that lumped together various acts of misconduct by Johnson. Though seven Republicans opposed the new article, the House majority approved it.

Johnson assembled a remarkable team of lawyers, led by Henry Stanbery, who resigned as Attorney General to lead his defense in the Senate. The team included a who's who of prominent American lawyers, including William Evarts, who had prosecuted Jefferson Davis for treason and also distinguished himself as an advocate before the Supreme Court (and had been on Lincoln's short list for consideration as a cabinet official); Jeremiah Black, a former senator from Pennsylvania who had served as James Buchanan's Attorney

General and whose Supreme Court nomination fell a single vote shy of confirmation in 1861; and Benjamin Curtis, who resigned from the Supreme Court to protest the Court's decision in *Dred Scott v. Sandford*[8] upholding a constitutional right for people to own slaves.

As the first impeachment and trial of a president, Johnson's case was closely followed by the public and marked a series of constitutional firsts. The House's impeachment articles against Johnson were the first formally drafted by the House against a president, and the House, having approved articles of impeachment, appointed for the first time a set of House Managers to prosecute the case for convicting and removing the president in the Senate. Now that those articles had been delivered to the Senate, that chamber had its first chance to draft rules for presidential impeachment trials, the Chief Justice prepared for the first time to preside over a presidential impeachment, and senators for the first time would have their chance to vote on whether to convict and remove a sitting president. The historical and constitutional significance of nearly every move was lost on no one.

II

With the House's impeachment articles against Johnson firmly in its grasp, the Senate moved swiftly to organize itself. It appointed a committee of seven—six Republicans and one Democrat, Reverdy Johnson, Zachary Taylor's Attorney General—to recommend procedures for the impeachment trial. On February 29, the committee reported 24 proposed rules, and it chose to refer to the Senate when conducting an impeachment trial as a "high court of impeachment." A debate ensued, informed by a letter Chase had sent to the Senate in early March explaining why he believed it important to distinguish between the Senate as a legislature and the Senate as a court for trying impeachments. He cautioned the Senate that "the rules for the government of the proceedings of such a court should be framed only by the court itself."[9] The *New York Herald* reported that Chase's letter had the "same effect upon the senators that an exploding torpedo would have on a school of porpoises." While the Senate forwarded the letter to a committee, more than a few senators regarded the letter "as a piece of impertinence on the part of the chief justice," the *Herald* reported, adding that "the radical senators are already expressing regrets that they will be compelled to have him as a presiding officer during the trial." Reflecting the discontent of the Senate with Chase's impertinence, the committee discarded the language referring to "high court of impeachment." The point now was that the Senate sat as the Senate. The rules also provided that the Chief Justice, as the presiding officer, had the authority to rule on any questions of law, procedure, and evidence, but that his rulings could be overturned by a majority of the Senate. When some Radical Republicans (pushed in part by Chase himself) objected, the committee drafted a more ambiguous provision, which became the subject of debate later during the trial. The rules further provided guidelines for debate, allowing, among other things, each side an hour to argue questions of law.

On March 4, the Senate resolved itself into a committee of the whole, and the next day the Chief Justice arrived. He was accompanied by Justice Samuel Nelson, the senior associate justice on the Court, and a committee of three senators. Justice Nelson administered the oath to the Chief Justice. With everyone standing, the Chief Justice then administered the oath to each senator—until Senator Benjamin Wade's turn. Senator Thomas Hendricks of Indiana objected that Wade should not be allowed to take an oath and otherwise participate because, as Senate Pro Tempore, Wade stood to become president if Johnson were removed (Johnson had no vice president). While the Senate quickly adjourned to deliberate, and the forty-four senators vigorously engaged in the debate over the question (with some arguing only the senator himself should decide on whether he is disqualified and others suggesting that at least some of them had conflicts of interest of one kind or another), the debate shifted to disagreements over Chase's comments on March 4 that the Senate had not yet adopted rules and none would apply unless it approved them. Twenty-four senators backed Chase's position in a vote, while 20 disagreed. After more debate, Hendricks withdrew his motion. After Chase declared the Senate in session as a court of impeachment, the Senate followed his suggestion and adopted, sitting as a court of impeachment, the rules it had previously approved as a legislature. The next day, Wade took the oath, and President Johnson was ordered to appear before the Senate a week later, on March 13.

On that date, Johnson's trial began. While congressional proceedings in that era were largely conducted behind closed doors, the Senate arranged for 800 people to sit in the galleries. Johnson's lawyers' first move was to request a forty-day period during which they would have the chance to formulate responses to the articles of impeachment. On behalf of the House Managers, Bingham vigorously opposed the motion, prompting Stanbery to turn to the Chief Justice and complain that "a case of the greatest magnitude we have ever had, is, as to time, to be treated as if it were a case before a police court, to be put through with railroad speed on the first day that the criminal appears!" The ensuing confusion over whether Chase should rule—as opposed to the Senate itself—prompted senators to adjourn in confusion. Two hours later, senators returned with the judgment that Johnson's lawyers had 10 days in which to file their answers to the impeachment charges. With Republicans united in opposition to the request, the Senate voted 26 to 25 to reject Bingham's request that the trial begin on the day the answer was filed. Butler promptly objected to Stanbery's characterization of the trial and Johnson himself: "Sir," he said to Chase, "who is the criminal—I beg pardon for the word—the respondent at the bar?" The Senate ruled the trial should begin as soon as possible after the House Managers filed their response to Johnson's lawyers' answers.

On March 23, the president's counsel filed their answers and introduced their case. The first impeachment article charged Johnson with violating the Tenure in Office Act by firing Stanton. The second alleged Johnson had violated the Act by naming Lorenzo Thomas to take Stanton's place. The third impeachment article declared that Johnson had violated the

Constitution by appointing Thomas to a post that was not vacant. The fourth article charged Johnson with conspiring with Thomas to prevent Stanton from holding office. Fifth, the articles charged Johnson and Thomas with conspiring to violate the Tenure in Office Act. The sixth article alleged that Johnson and Thomas had used force to seize the Office of the Secretary of War, and the seventh basically reiterated the charge in the sixth. The eighth article of impeachment charged Johnson with having violated the Tenure in Office Act by ordering Thomas to seize the property of the war secretary's office, and the ninth alleged that Johnson had violated federal law by ordering the general in charge of defending Washington, William Emory, to disregard federal mandates requiring that military orders "issued through the General of the Army" ignore Grant's orders. That left the tenth and eleventh articles, which together charged Johnson with having breached the public trust placed in him as president. Evarts and Curtis outlined their case: that Johnson was entitled as president to appoint or remove all executive officers "for cause to be judged by the President alone"; that the Tenure in Office Act did not apply to Johnson or Stanton because the Act provided that the cabinet officers who were subject to it for the term of the president who appointed them (Lincoln in this case) plus one month; that Johnson had used only peaceful means to "vindicate his authority as President of the United States"; that Johnson was free to speak his mind as he pleased as president; and that the eleventh article contained no specific charges.[10] They concluded with a request for a thirty-day delay. The Senate rejected the request, voting 41 to 12. Evarts then asked for a continuance of whatever length of time the Senate deemed reasonable, and the Senate adjourned for debate. The next day, the Senate reconvened to take up the question of how much more time to give to the defense for preparation, but Senator Charles Sumner of Massachusetts requested that the Senate trial proceed at once. The Senate denied his request (29–23), took a short break, and returned with its judgment that the trial would begin in six days.

A week later, the trial began in earnest. Butler presented the House Managers' case against Johnson: Over the course of three hours, he argued (1) the Constitution did not require that impeachment be based on some indictable crime; (2) that impeachment could be based on abuse of powers; (3) the Senate was not a court when sitting to try impeachments but instead was "bound by no law, either statute or common, which may limit your constitutional prerogative"; and (4) the burden of proof for criminal trials—proof beyond a reasonable doubt—did not apply to these proceedings.[11] Each argument closely tracked the origins and design of the federal impeachment process.

The next day, Johnson's lawyers presented their defense. First, they argued that impeachable offenses must be indictable offenses. For principal support, they reminded senators that the Constitution expressly mentioned "crimes" and "misdemeanors" (a set of crimes). Second, they argued that Stanton was not covered by the Tenure in Office Act. They read the act as protecting Stanton from removal only through the term of the president who had appointed him. Because Johnson was now president and because he had not appointed Stanton, the act did not bar him from removing a cabinet member for any reason. Third, they argued that, even if Stanton were covered by the law, it was hardly clear and therefore should not be a basis for removing a president from office. It was unfair to turn that lack of clarity against the president. Fourth, they argued that, even if Stanton were covered by the Tenure in Office Act, the law breached the president's discretion over how "to take care that the laws be faithfully executed." It was up to Johnson, not Congress, on how best to enforce the law.

When the House Managers called their first witness, Walter Burleigh, who was a friend of General Thomas, Stanbery objected that the testimony should not be allowed because it was irrelevant. Senators had already had some sharp exchanges over Chief Justice Chase's role, but the objection forced them to address the question again. For his part, Chief Justice Chase said that he agreed with Stanbery that he had the power to rule on the question. Senator Charles Drake, a Republican from Missouri, argued that Chase had no authority to make any such ruling, while Chase himself countered that it was traditional for presiding officers, particularly in courts, to wield such authority. Butler disagreed, arguing that allowing the Chief Justice's rulings to stand unless overturned by the Senate meant the House Managers "cannot get the question we propose before the Senate unless through the courtesy of some senator." He argued further that, because Chase was not a senator, he should not be allowed any kind of vote in the proceedings. The matter, however, was put to the Senate, which split, 25 to 25—and Chase moved quickly to cast the tiebreaking vote in his own favor. It was a blatant move for Chase to enhance not only his own power as presiding officer but also his presidential prospects.

When given a chance, Chase did what he could to help Johnson's side. Chase was worried that removing Johnson would elevate Benjamin Wade, the Senate Pro Tempore, to the presidency. Chase wanted that job for himself; though he adamantly denied such rumors circulating in newspapers, that is exactly what he wanted. When Senator Sumner requested a vote on whether Chase should be allowed a vote in the proceedings, his motion failed by six votes. The Senate then compromised, 31 to 19, on a rule providing the Chief Justice had the right to rule "on all questions of evidence and incidental questions" unless a member of the Senate asked to have the full Senate consider the question. When Sumner later asked Senator George Edwards of Vermont why he had voted against Sumner's motion, Edwards replied, "Mr. Chase was already very angry. So you see how constitutional questions are decided."[12]

On Thursday, April 9, Benjamin Curtis, the former justice, led Johnson's defense in putting on its case in full. Though he kept his promise that his remarks would be "dry work," he returned to the argument made earlier in the proceedings that there was nothing ambiguous about the Tenure in Office Act's provision that cabinet members "shall hold their offices respectively for and during the term of the President by whom they have been appointed and for one month thereafter, subject to removal by and with the advice and consent of the Senate." Stanton was merely serving out the remainder of Lincoln's term: "The necessary conclusion that the tenure-of-office of a secretary here described is a tenure during the term of service of the President by whom he was appointed; that it was not the intention of Congress to compel a President of the United States to continue in office a Secretary not appointed by himself." Since Johnson had not appointed Stanton, Johnson could not be compelled to keep him.[13] While Curtis's argument appeared to some as circular because he was arguing both that the Act did not apply to Stanton but that Johnson had violated the Act with good intentions, it did not stop him from continuing the next day to rebut each of the other charges made against Johnson.

On Friday, April 10, and Saturday, April 11, Johnson's team proceeded to call witnesses, but the questioning over the next few days bogged down procedurally as Chief Justice Chase presumed that he had the power to make rulings on witnesses and admissibility of evidence, though the Senate rules made clear that the ultimate decision maker on such questions was the Senate itself. On April 16, Senator Sumner moved that all testimony should be admitted into evidence without argument and that its weight should be determined by the Senate. The motion was quickly tabled.

The next day, Chief Justice Chase's luck began to run out. Evarts called to the stand Gideon Welles, who had served as Lincoln's secretary of the navy and was a strong Johnson ally. When Evarts asked Welles when Johnson decided to fire Stanton, Butler objected that the answer was irrelevant. Chase ruled the testimony was relevant. After lengthy debate, the Senate overruled him, 26 to 23, in what Chase took as a stinging rebuke. Debate continued into the following day. For a second time, the Senate voted not to allow the testimony, though this time by a wider margin, 29 to 20, an even sharper rebuke to Chase than before.

Given what appeared to be the Senate's obstinance against the testimony of Welles, defense lawyers dropped their plans to call other cabinet secretaries as witnesses. Though Chase was visibly angry, he did not dare for the remainder of the trial to test wills with the Senate.

By the time the trial resumed on April 20, Henry Stanbery had resigned from the defense because of poor health (though he would return near the end of the trial). Johnson's other lawyers announced they had finished presenting their case, but senators erupted in debate over how many lawyers from each side could make concluding remarks. It took several days before each side rested. Subsequently, the Senate convened to consider procedural questions and to hear the final arguments from both sides. A closed-door meeting for the Senate to debate the charges was set for mid-May.

When the time came, the House Managers and lawyers for Johnson focused on whether Johnson was serving out Lincoln's term or his own. The House Managers argued that Johnson was not elected president in his own right but instead was merely completing the remainder of Lincoln's term and thus the plain language of the Tenure in Office Act applied to him. In response, the president's lawyers argued that (1) if the House Managers were correct in their reading of the Act, it was a highly debatable reading and thus not an appropriate basis for removing a president; (2) the president had the inherent power to remove executive branch officials at will to fulfill his constitutional duties; and (3) the president was entitled to have the courts adjudicate whether he had the unilateral power to remove a cabinet officer or other executive official. If the president could not unilaterally remove a cabinet member who had lost his trust or was not doing as he requested, he no longer had control over the executive branch. Congress was effectively being allowed to control how he performed his constitutional duties.

As the trial was winding down, Chase's attitudes about his role had shifted. Throughout the trial, he had made no secret that he found the arguments from lawyers on both sides to be tedious, writing to a friend of his, James Pike, that there was "too much talking by half."[14] In early May, Chase decided that he would not "charge the jury" as he might in a court of law. He explained in a letter to John Van Buren that he was not a member of the court of impeachment but was merely its presiding officer. "Even if the chief justice were," he wrote, "a member of the court, he would have no right to charge the other members of the court; he could only express his opinion in common with them." He said his role was limited to "rule preliminarily on questions of evidence" and should, if requested, "express his opinion on any other question."[15]

Chase may have just been saying these things to curry favor, or perhaps he was responding to other influences. Throughout the trial, he had been meeting informally with senators, and on May 12 he had dinner with several senators who were disposed to acquit Johnson. Chase had more than one such party at his home. At the time, the *New York Herald* reported that it was perhaps only a "trifling circumstance, but the impeachers take it sadly to heart." The *Washington Morning Chronicle* reported that Chase had "resorted to an extraordinary amount of dinner diplomacy, and long drives with doubtful senators, to defeat impeachment."[16]

On May 16, the Senate convened for its final vote. Senator George Williams, who had left the Democratic Party to become a Republican, asked that that the Senate first be allowed to vote on the eleventh impeachment article. The Senate agreed, voting 34 to 19 in favor. The Chief Justice proceeded to ask each senator for his vote on Johnson's guilt. In the final tally, 35 senators voted to convict Johnson on the eleventh article, while 19 senators voted to acquit him. Chief Justice Chase declared: "Two-thirds not having pronounced guilty, the President is, therefore, acquitted on that article." The Senate then voted 32 to 21 to adjourn, but when the Senate reconvened, its vote on the second article of impeachment was the same as its vote on the eleventh article. The vote on the third article was the same as it had been for the two previous articles. The Senate then voted to approve Williams's motion to adjourn once and for all. The outcome was clear: Senators were not going to vote differently on any other article. Johnson had been acquitted, albeit by a margin of a single vote.

III

Several lessons and ramifications can be discerned from the trial and acquittal of President Andrew Johnson. First, the acquittal, combined with the Supreme Court's decision in 1922 to strike down a law that was similar to the Tenure in Office Act,[17] can be understood as affirming the principles that presidents have inherent unilateral powers to fire cabinet officers *and* to make different policy choices than Congress based on their constitutional commitments.

Second, in his book on the impeachment and trials of Supreme Court Justice Samuel Chase and President Johnson, Chief Justice William Rehnquist speculated on their ramifications for future presidents and justices. He argued that Johnson's acquittal illuminated the scope of impeachable offenses for presidents. Said Rehnquist, "It was not any technical violation of the law that would suffice, but it was the sort of violation of the law that would in itself justify removal from office." The Chief Justice did not say anything more about what violations might qualify to justify removal, nor could he have done so, since the context and gravity of the offense are the crucial elements of impeachable offenses. Nevertheless, Chief Justice Rehnquist added: "The importance of these acquittals can hardly be overstated. With respect to the chief executive, they have meant as to policies he sought to pursue, he would be answerable only to the country as a whole in the quadrennial presidential elections, and not to Congress through the process of impeachment."[18]

Third, the Johnson trial raised concerns about whether senators can rise above petty partisan politics during such proceedings and instead engage in high-minded politics. In his Pulitzer Prize–winning book *Profiles in Courage*, John F. Kennedy featured Senator Edmond Ross of Kansas as casting the pivotal vote to acquit Johnson and subsequently losing his Senate seat as punishment. More recent scholarship suggests Ross, a Republican, did not go against his party's wishes for altruistic reasons but instead in exchange for bribes. Nor was he the only senator to do so. Indeed, senators throughout the trial were making backroom deals, meeting with Chase or Johnson or sometimes both, meeting (sometimes on the Senate floor) with and being investigated by George Wilkes, a newspaper editor frequently charged with blackmail and who worked closely with Butler, talking with the press, and communicating with party leaders or constituents back home or in Washington. A subsequent investigation led by Butler revealed a broad range of dubious illegal activity not always hidden behind the scenes, though the report itself was skewed to fit Butler's perception of events. As David Stewart suggests in his book on the Johnson trial, there were few if any genuine heroes.[19]

Despite the Constitution's safeguards, most senators failed to rise to the occasion. When the Constitution was amended to alter the selection of senators from state legislatures to voters in their respective states, senators became more prone to public (and other kinds of) pressure, including bribery by means other than just money—the promise of support from the party, the president, or others for future office, for example. Such pressures could be—and are—placed on House members, too, though there is nothing to suggest that James Garfield, who voted as a member of the House to impeach Johnson, did anything inappropriate.

The fourth lesson involves the role of the Chief Justice. By nearly any standard, Chase was aggressive, at least in the first weeks of the trial, and intent on being more than a ceremonial figure: He tried to consolidate his power over the proceedings not only to perform as a judge in a real trial might but also to service his political ambitions. Yet in the end, Chase proved to be a paper tiger. Once senators made it clear, in both the rules and practice, that any ruling by Chase could be appealed to them for affirmation or overruling, Chase learned that the senators, not the Presiding Officer, were the crucial decision makers over all procedural and substantive questions. He admitted as much at the end of the trial.

The final matter involves the question whether Johnson could or should have been impeached. The answer is likely "yes." How far does a president's discretion to execute the laws faithfully extend? Does it extend to refusing to execute at all a duly enacted law the president happens to disagree with? If presidents can do this without fear of impeachment, they establish themselves as the principal authorities over both the enforcement and making of law.

As with pretty much everything else, there is likely a breaking point. The question becomes not whether a president may be impeached, convicted, and removed for not executing the law (which, by virtue of the Supremacy Clause, is the "supreme law of the land") but when. And that question, as every other presidential impeachment has shown us, is left for Congress to decide.

[3]

Richard Nixon and Watergate

Over the next century and more, few people took seriously the prospect of presidential impeachment. Johnson's acquittal might have sent the signal that impeachment was ineffective in a case dealing with one of America's most unpopular presidents and thus should pose no worry for more popular (or craftier) presidents.

This is not to say there were no scandals. Indeed, there were several. In 1923, President Warren Harding became enraged and upset at rumors of corruption throughout his administration. When he discovered that Attorney General Harry Daugherty might have been involved in the scandals, Harding physically attacked and began choking him. The president had to be forcibly pulled off for fear he might kill Daugherty. When Harding flew cross-country with Secretary of Commerce Herbert Hoover, Hoover recalled Harding's telling him, "If you knew of a great scandal in our administration, would you for the good of the country and the party expose it publicly or would you bury it?" Hoover said he would publicize it, but Harding appeared dubious. Harding died shortly thereafter from a heart attack. When Vice President Calvin Coolidge became president, he fired Daugherty and wasted no time in agreeing to authorize a congressional inquiry and to back it regardless of the findings.

The different attitudes of Harding and Coolidge illustrate the two approaches presidents can take with respect to scandal or misconduct at a high level in their administrations. The public rewarded Coolidge's openness to investigation (and the continued strong economy) by electing him to the presidency in his own right in 1924. Yet Harding's instincts were not unique; as the nation learned several decades later, the coverup can be worse than the crimes.

The case in point was Richard Nixon. Unlike Johnson, Nixon had been elected to two consecutive terms as president, the second by the largest margin of victory in the Electoral College until 1984. Nixon, a Republican stalwart, had achievements to tout, particularly in his run for reelection, including the enactments of the Clean Air Act and Clean Water Act, restoring law and order in the aftermath of the excesses of the 1960s, and bringing the Vietnam War to an end. Perhaps most important, he appointed four justices, which transformed the Supreme Court from the liberal bastion it had been since the 1930s to a conservative one that promised to be less tolerant of criminal defendants. Yet Nixon lacked the warmth and charisma of many other commanders in chief, was naturally (and sometimes virulently) distrustful of people (especially his opponents), and harbored abhorrent attitudes about Jews and minorities that did not come fully to light until after he left the presidency. Five days before his second inauguration, five burglars pled guilty to the Watergate break-in, and the specter of Watergate—fueled in part by the burglars' defense that Nixon had ordered them to do it—haunted Nixon throughout the rest of the year.

A presidency often tests limits, and Nixon tested the limits of his office in a series of brazen acts in his first and second terms. The historian Arthur Schlesinger, Jr., coined the phrase increasingly associated with Nixon in the title of his book, *The Imperial Presidency*, published in 1973, which examined the rise in presidential power over the course of American history. In his brazenness, Nixon was the catalyst for his own undoing.

It began with what many historians have called a "second-rate burglary." In fact, it was a burglary of the Democratic Party's headquarters in the Watergate Hotel on June 17, 1972, in the middle of the 1972 presidential election campaign. When one burglar was discovered with a piece of paper with a phone number at the White House, the *Washington Post* reporters Carl Bernstein and Bob Woodward pounced. They used every journalistic means possible to track down the source of the money that had paid for the burglary. Besides their investigation, the Department of Justice, over Nixon's objection, appointed a special prosecutor, Archibald Cox, a widely respected labor law professor at Harvard Law School who had also been Solicitor General under John F. Kennedy. Both the House and the Senate opened investigations into the Watergate break-in to determine, as Republican Senator Howard Baker repeatedly asked, "What did the President know, and when did he know it?" Thus, Nixon was being investigated on three parallel tracks: by a special prosecutor, the House, and the Senate.

Over the course of more than a year, the congressional and special prosecutor investigations bore fruit, which made matters increasingly worse for Nixon. He allowed his White House counsel, John Dean, to testify before the Senate, but his testimony blew up in Nixon's face when Dean admitted that he had discussed the cover-up 35 times with Nixon and that he had participating in the illegal cover-up himself. Even worse for Nixon, Alexander Butterfield, one of Nixon's assistants, informed the Senate on July 16 that there was a taping system within the White House to record the president's conversations. Nixon promptly disconnected the taping mechanisms and refused to turn the tapes over to either the special prosecutor or to the Senate Committee investigating the break-in.

The special prosecutor subpoenaed the tapes, but Nixon refused to comply. His defiance provoked Special Prosecutor Cox to go to court. After Cox secured rulings, from District Judge John Sirica and a federal appellate court, ordering Nixon to comply with the subpoena, Nixon fired Cox, prompting both Attorney General Elliott Richardson (who had promised in his confirmation hearings to appoint a special prosecutor to investigate Watergate) and the deputy attorney general to resign on the evening of Saturday, October 20, 1973. Earlier that same month, on October 10, Vice President Spiro Agnew had resigned in disgrace because of revelations (and a state indictment) that he had committed crimes when he was governor of Maryland.

By the end of the year, Nixon was plainly in trouble. His protestation on November 17, 1973, that "I am not a crook" to a meeting of Associated Press editors did nothing to instill confidence among Americans that he was not. Matters worsened over the next few months as seven high-level officials, including Attorney General John Mitchell, resigned in disgrace (and under indictment) for their involvement in various scandals. When the House and Senate each agreed near the end of the year to the appointment of Gerald Ford, Republican leader in the House, as vice president, members of Congress knew he might soon be president—the first time ever someone not elected as president or vice president was eligible for, and would assume, the highest office in the land.

Several other intervening developments unfolded that did not bode well for Nixon. In March 1974, Judge Sirica dealt Nixon another blow. Previously, he had ruled that Nixon had to comply with a subpoena to turn over various tapes to the criminal defendants whose defense was that they were operating under presidential orders. In those earlier proceedings, Nixon had been named an unindicted co-conspirator with the Watergate burglars. But on March 18, Sirica shared the grand jury's sealed report with the House Judiciary Committee. The materials consisted of nearly all the Special Prosecutor's evidence of Nixon's culpability. While the Special Prosecutor had no authority to make recommendations to the Judiciary Committee, there was no law precluding it from giving the committee such details of Nixon's culpability; this report became known as the "Road Map."

The referral made sense under the circumstances at that time. The new special prosecutor, Leon Jaworski, appointed on November 1, 1973, due to intense pressure applied to Nixon after he fired Cox, would adopt the opinion of the Justice Department that a sitting president was likely not indictable for any criminal activity. The reasoning was that criminally investigating or prosecuting a president would paralyze the operations of the executive branch, as the president would be distracted by the threat of possible imprisonment. Thus, besides in prosecuting various White House officials other than Nixon, Jaworski believed any evidence of Nixon's culpability in serious misconduct should be considered first and foremost by the House Judiciary Committee. Jaworski was not fast, but he was dogged: On April 16, his office subpoenaed 64 tapes. Nixon released some edited ones, but the House Judiciary Committee and the Special Prosecutor did not trust his edits and wanted ten of the tapes themselves.

Neither the House nor the Senate slowed down their investigations as the Supreme Court was being drawn into deciding the Watergate Tapes case. The courts already had become the fourth institution reviewing Nixon's misconduct. What ensued was the first time in history that a president faced the prospect of being held accountable for his misconduct on multiple fronts. Eventually, every institution but the presidency came out a winner.

I

By the time the Supreme Court heard arguments in *United States v. Nixon*, 418 U.S. 683 (1974), on July 8, Nixon had little hope of completing his second term. With every revelation of misconduct, the prospects of impeachment by the House seemed to increase, and his popularity plummeted. At the time of Nixon's inauguration for his second term on

January 20, 1973, his popularity was nearly 70%. Less than three months later in April, 83% of the American people indicated they had heard of the Watergate scandal; after Nixon accepted the resignations of top aides John Ehrlichman and H. R. Haldeman on April 30, Nixon's popularity fell to 48%. When the televised hearings of the Senate looking into possible misconduct on Nixon's part began in May, 71% of the American people said Nixon was culpable for his involvement in the Watergate break-in (and other misconduct that was coming to light). Yet only 26% of Americans at that time thought Nixon should be impeached.[1]

Nixon was not so naïve as to think the Supreme Court's decision in the Watergate tapes case would have no impact on his popularity or, more important, the prospect of impeachment. While he was publicly arguing that as president he was entitled not to share confidential information about his own activities with another branch, most people suspected that Nixon was withholding the tapes as part of a cover-up. There were strong suspicions the tape had some "smoking gun" of Nixon's misconduct. Thus, as public attention focused on the Court, it was understood that something more than just the president's entitlement to executive privilege (the formal doctrine entitling presidents to keep confidential information produced by them or on their behalf) was at stake. Nixon's future—and the future of the presidency itself—was at risk.

In advising Nixon on the arguments that should be made on his behalf before the Supreme Court, his counsel James St. Clair warned him against asserting his boldest claim that presidents were entitled to an absolute executive privilege—or immunity from being forced to disclose to the public, Congress, or anyone else anything that they (the presidents) deemed confidential. St. Clair understood that every president before Nixon had made the claim, which undoubtedly was strong historical support, but any loss by Nixon would be a loss for the presidency itself. Courts had never before ruled on the scope of presidents' executive privilege. If the Court ruled in favor of Nixon, then he and all future presidents would have that decision on their side in arguing in whatever venue, such as Congress, that they were entitled to an absolute executive privilege. But if Nixon lost, the presidency itself could be deprived of an important protection on which it had relied in dealings with Congress and lower courts.

Nixon insisted that St. Clair make the argument. He was banking on his four appointees to the Court to be receptive to his arguments.

They were not. Nixon had vowed to appoint strict "law and order" justices who would not coddle criminal defendants or find previously unheard-of rights and procedures to undo the convictions of guilty parties and leave them scot-free to commit further crimes. Ironically, three of those newly appointed justices—Chief Justice Warren Burger, Harry Blackmun, and Lewis Powell—were prepared to uphold the rule of law against the president himself and to ensure that no one, not even Nixon, was above the law. The fourth—William Rehnquist—recused himself from the case because, prior to his appointment, he had advised Nixon on the arguments in the case.

In less than a month after hearing the arguments, the Court released its decision in an opinion by the Chief Justice, and it was unanimous—all eight justices sitting in the case ruled against Nixon. The "law and order" justices lined up against Nixon in joining Burger's opinion, which made two basic points. First, the Court rejected Nixon's claim that it should not adjudicate his refusal to comply with judicial subpoenas. The Court emphasized, quoting from *Marbury v. Madison*, that it is the "duty of this Court 'to say what the law is' with respect to the claim of privilege presented in this case."[2]

Second, the Supreme Court rejected Nixon's claim of an entitlement to absolute executive privilege. Nixon based his claim on the needs for the presidency to be independent from review or monitoring by the other branches and for people working for or with the president to feel free to share opinions and conversations with the president about policy without the fear of those remarks or suggestions becoming public. The Court found neither of those grounds justified an absolute privilege in this case:

> The President's need for complete candor and objectivity from advisers calls for great deference from the courts. However, when the privilege depends solely on the broad, undifferentiated claim of public interest in the confidentiality of such conversations, a confrontation with other values arises. Absent a claim of need to protect military, diplomatic, or sensitive national security secrets, we find it difficult to accept the argument that even the very important interest

in confidentiality of Presidential communications is significantly diminished by production of such material for in camera inspection with all the protection that a district court will be obliged to provide.

Further, the Court observed, "The impediment that an absolute, unqualified privilege would place in the way of the primary constitutional duty of the Judiciary to do justice in criminal prosecutions would plainly conflict with the functions of the courts under Article III." Nixon had argued that the absolute privilege was necessary to ensure the presidency operated on equal footing with the other branches. But, the Court explained, an absolute privilege would actually give the presidency primacy over the judiciary since the latter would never be able to review presidential communications for any reason, including discussions of illegal misconduct. Thus, the Court recognized that the president had only a *qualified* (not absolute) executive privilege subject to courts' balancing of the competing considerations in any given case.

While the Court conceded that presidents were entitled to presumptive privileges (out of deference and the expectation of presidents operating in good faith), the Court determined that presidents could easily undermine the "ends of criminal justice" and the "integrity of the judicial system and public confidence in the system." The Court stressed that the president's claim undermined every citizen's "right to the production of all evidence at a criminal trial." Thus, the Court concluded that "when the ground for asserting privilege as to subpoenaed materials sought for use in a criminal trial is based only on the generalized interest in confidentiality, it cannot prevail over the fundamental demands of due process in the fair administration of justice. The generalized assertion of privilege must yield to the demonstrated, specific need for evidence in a pending criminal trial." While Nixon drew attention to statements made by Chief Justice John Marshall that presidents should not be treated like ordinary citizens, the Court emphasize that "Marshall's statement cannot be read to mean in any sense that the President is above the law."[3]

Had Nixon prevailed in asserting entitlement to absolute executive privilege, the presidency would effectively be above the law. Presidents would be able to clothe themselves in an impenetrable veil of secrecy from the courts. Indeed, Nixon's arguments did not allow that executive privilege could be abused. The question of how that claim would fare in the impeachment process would be tested in the few weeks following the Court's decision.

II

The Supreme Court's decision added momentum to the Special Prosecutor and congressional investigations that were already under way. Nixon initially hesitated to comply with the Court's order, but he soon realized he had no choice: Intense public, media, and congressional scrutiny, along with the advice of his lawyers, convinced Nixon to comply. Any further defiance guaranteed his ouster.

More than five months before the Supreme Court released its opinion, impeachment hearings had begun. On February 6, the House, voting 410 to 4, had approved a formal impeachment inquiry into Nixon's misconduct. Relations between Democratic and Republican leaders were not so fractured then that members could not work with, or respect, each other. When House Judiciary Committee Chair Peter Rodino, a Democrat, promised "let us now proceed with such care and decency and thoroughness and honor that the vast majority of the American people, and their children after them, will say, 'This was the right course, there was no other way,'" House Minority Leader John Rhodes said, "good with me."

On February 9, the committee released a report on the constitutional grounds for presidential impeachment that its staff had already been working on. John Doar, a Republican who had worked in both the Kennedy and Johnson administrations, was the lead counsel for the committee and had been given a free hand in assembling the staff. Though there were two staffs, one Democratic and one Republican, Doar insisted that its work be as evenhanded as possible. Assisted by Yale historian C. Vann Woodward, the staff—with such young lawyers as Hillary Clinton and William Weld (later governor of Massachusetts) and Zoe Lofgren (later elected to the House from California)[4]—published a 64-page report titled "Constitutional Grounds for Presidential Impeachment." The report remains the gold standard on the background and history of federal impeachment in this country.[5]

Among its most important conclusions, the report determined that an impeachable offense did not have to be a criminal infraction. Rather, the report found, "The Framers did not write a fixed standard. Instead[,] they adopted from English history a standard sufficiently general and flexible to meet future circumstances and events, the nature of which they could not foresee." The "scope of impeachment was not viewed narrowly [by the framers]," the report stated. "It was intended to provide a check on the President through impeachment, but not to make him dependent on the unbridled will of the Congress."

The report went further to find that impeachable offenses fell into three different categories: first, those "exceeding the powers of the office in derogation of those of another branch"; second, "behaving in a manner grossly incompatible with the proper functions and purpose of the office"; and third, "employing the power of the office for an improper purpose or personal gain." Notably, the report determined that "criminality" was not a required element of an impeachable offense. "The emphasis," the report explained, "has been on the significant effects of the conduct—undermining the integrity of the office, disregarding of constitutional duties and oath of office, arrogation of power, abuse of the governmental process, adverse impact on the system of government. Clearly, these effects can be brought about in ways not anticipated by the criminal law." In England, colonial America, and at the time of the founding, the report added, impeachment had been designed as a process distinct from the criminal system; the latter was intended "to control individual conduct," but impeachment was intended to protect the nation from abuses that were not addressed in the criminal law. Nixon's lawyers and supportive Republican members of the House countered that these grounds were too broad and murky and instead suggested that impeachable offenses had to be of "a very serious nature."[6] Of course, this standard was hardly more concrete than the grounds specified in the report.

Moreover, the grand jury materials that Sirica had shared with the committee on March 1 had been assembled by Jaworski's team. Jaworski understood that his office was not authorized or empowered to make impeachment recommendations to the House, but no law precluded him from seeking the permission from Judge Sirica to share the evidence his office had gathered that demonstrated Nixon's culpability. The evidence consisted of 800 pages of documents and 13 tape recordings of Nixon's Oval Office conversations. The Special Prosecutor included among the materials a 55-page memo, the "Road Map." As one of the authors later described the content of the memo, it made the "conclusion that the President of the United States took part in a criminal conspiracy . . . inescapable."[7] Most important, the road map set forth the evidence that supported impeachment charges against the president. All the House Judiciary Committee had to do was to follow the evidence. Though it was not bound to do so, it did, calling a string of witnesses throughout the weeks leading up to the Court's decision.

Later on the same day that the Court issued its opinion, the House Judiciary Committee held a meeting to consider the grounds for impeaching Richard Nixon. The hearing was filled with spirited debate, but no speech had more impact on the public's views of the subject than from a congresswoman in her first term, Barbara Jordan, the first woman and the first woman of color to hold a Texas seat in the House. Her 13-minute speech was riveting, as her strong, clear voice resonated throughout the chamber. "I am not going to sit here," she said, "and be an idle spectator to the diminution, the subversion, and the destruction, of the Constitution." She declared, "We know the nature of impeachment. . . . It is chiefly designed for the President and his ministers be somehow called to account. It is designed to 'bridle' the Executive if he engages in excesses. . . . The framers confided in the Congress the power, if need be, to remove the President in order to strike a balance between a President swollen with power and grown tyrannical, and preservation of the independence of the Executive." She walked the committee through some of the evidence demonstrating Nixon's misconduct and reminded both them and anyone watching of James Madison's statement to the Virginia ratifying convention: "If the President be connected in any suspicious manner with any person and there be grounds to believe that he will shelter him, he may be impeached." Besides quoting Justice Story and Woodrow Wilson, she turned again to Madison, who had told the Constitutional Convention: "A president is impeachable if he attempts to subvert the Constitution." Under that standard, she said, there was no doubt Nixon had committed impeachable offenses: "Has the President committed offenses, and planned, and directed, and acquiesced in a course of conduct which the Constitution will not tolerate? That's the question.

We know that. We know the question. We should now forthwith proceed to answer the question. It is reason, not passion, which must guide our deliberations, guide our debate, guide our decision."[8]

Three days after the Supreme Court issued its opinion, the House Judiciary Committee voted 27 to 11 to recommend to the full House its first impeachment article charging Nixon with obstruction of justice. Two days later, the committee approved a second article of impeachment, this one charging Nixon with having abused his powers by ordering the heads of the FBI, CIA, and IRS to harass his political enemies. On July 30, the committee approved its third article of impeachment, which charged Nixon with having failed to comply with four legislative subpoenas requesting specific White House tapes. Though the House Judiciary Committee had been investigating other possible misconduct, such as tax fraud, it limited itself to recommending these three articles to the House, presumably because they were the strongest and had the clearest, closest connection between the misconduct and the president's duties.

Over the next few days, support for impeachment grew in the House as Nixon scrambled to find a way out. The release of the tapes before the Court's decision hurt Nixon more than they helped, including a recording of a conversation within the White House on June 20, 1972, which contained a gap of 18 and a half minutes. But the tape released by the White House on August 5 sealed his fate: It became known as the "smoking gun" because it included a conversation between Haldeman and Ehrlichman discussing a plan to block the

FBI. Though later clarified as a conversation about blocking an FBI investigation into a Nixon donor, Nixon publicly apologized for having misled the nation about when he had been told about the involvement of the White House in the Watergate scandal.

On August 7, 1974, Nixon met with Republican leaders John Rhodes from the House and Barry Goldwater and Hugh Scott from the Senate. Nixon asked them about the level of his support within both chambers. It is a myth that they urged him to resign. In fact, they told him he had little support in either chamber, Goldwater going so far as telling Nixon that he thought Nixon had at most support from nine senators (well below the number he needed to secure an acquittal in the Senate). John Rhodes later said he had the impression Nixon was already preparing to resign, but he and Goldwater strenuously denied ever having made any suggestion to Nixon on what he should do.

Nixon prepared to leave the presidency rather than face the ignominy of becoming the first president convicted and removed from office by the Senate. On the evening of August 8, Nixon delivered his last televised address. He told the American people he intended to resign the next day. "By taking this action," he said, "I hope that I will have hastened the start of a process of healing which is so desperately needed in America." The next day, shortly before noon, Nixon had delivered a one-sentence letter to Vice President Ford informing him that he was resigning. Nixon and his family boarded a helicopter to leave the White House and return home to California.

After having taken the oath of office as president, Gerald Ford delivered his first televised address. He declared, "My fellow Americans, our long national nightmare is over."[9]

III

The conventional wisdom has been that Nixon's demise is the prime example of the system working as it should, and for the most part it is. The Special Prosecutor's office worked meticulously and well within the scope of its power to uncover and prosecute the people within the Nixon administration who had broken the law. In fact, 69 people were prosecuted and 48 convicted, including a vice president (Spiro Agnew), two Attorneys General (John Mitchell and Richard Kleindienst), White House counsel (John Dean), Chief of Staff (H. R. Haldeman), Secretary of Commerce (Maurice Stans), secretary to the president (Dwight Chapin), and deputy director of the Committee to Re-elect the President (Jeb Magruder). Both the House and Senate conducted investigations that became models for future inquiries into presidential or other high-level misconduct, though House leaders, including the members on the House Judiciary Committee, did not follow what they regarded as the Senate's less-than-exemplary practice of granting immunity in exchange for testimony.

Yet several significant constitutional questions persist in the aftermath of Nixon's resignation. The first has had to do with the resignation itself. Did the Watergate scandal, at least insofar as Nixon was concerned, demonstrate the utility of forced resignation rather than the effectiveness of impeachment? Indeed, is a forced resignation the best that can be expected from inquiries into presidential misconduct? What if presidents were not so inclined to resign?

Neither of the next two presidents who found themselves embroiled by impeachment proceedings—Bill Clinton and Donald Trump—were the resigning type. As best we can tell, neither thought for a moment of resigning, especially since neither faced a serious prospect of being criminally prosecuted while they were in office (as the Nixon Justice Department had authored the initial policy of treating presidents as immune to any such prosecutions while they were in office). Moreover, neither faced any serious possibility of conviction in the Senate. After all, what might Nixon have done if his party had united behind him, if not in the House then in the Senate? The Senate never would have been able to convict and remove him if more than a third of the senators opposed his ouster, and more than a third of the senators were Republican in Nixon's second term. Democrats and Republicans did not abandon Clinton or Trump, respectively, in the Senate. Without any serious prospect of conviction or prosecution, neither Clinton nor Trump had any incentive to resign.

Second, many scholars have regarded the third impeachment article against Nixon as the weakest. A prominent critique was that the president's refusal to comply with a legislative subpoena was likely not an impeachable offense. The reasoning was that ensuring the equality of the branches required allowing presidents the discretion to oppose subpoenas; they needed that freedom to protect the office from overreaching by the Congress. The Watergate tapes case could be read as answering only what happens when there is a conflict between the president and courts over executive privilege, but it said nothing about a conflict between presidents and Congress over whether a president had to comply with a legislative subpoena. Though a concern raised on behalf of more than one president has been whether Congress's directly subpoenaing a president is a direct challenge to his authority and stature, Thomas Jefferson, Nixon, and Bill Clinton complied with judicial subpoenas.

The more pertinent question is what should happen to presidents who refuse to comply with subpoenas for information that they alone control. If they are not obliged to comply with such subpoenas and their defiance is not in itself impeachable, how is it possible to hold presidents accountable for their misconduct through the impeachment process? If presidents have the power to block Congress from securing information that the president has about his own misconduct, then their future as presidents depends on the extent to which people within their own administration refuse to work with Congress or to disclose the information to other authorities. If, for example, a president sanctioned the assassination of a foreign leader in contravention of a congressional directive otherwise but can keep all pertinent information in his possession, Congress must then rely on people close to the president to report his misconduct. The impossibility of treating noncompliance with lawful legislative subpoenas effectively gives presidents another advantage in the impeachment process in addition to the high threshold that the Constitution requires for a conviction in the Senate.

Personally, I do not believe that the United States Constitution was designed or intended to give presidents that much protection. Surely, the Constitution allows Congress to hold hearings to hold to account the Chief Justice, or any associate justices—or, for that matter, cabinet secretaries, the vice president, or members of Congress, including the House Speaker or Senate Majority Leader. Why, then, does the president become the sole official immune to such scrutiny? The answer, in whatever form it takes, is that the president must be special. But what makes a president so special that, in effect, this one official can easily evade—and undermine—the very process designed to hold the president accountable for misconduct while in office? As far as the Constitution is concerned, it does not make presidents special when it comes to hiding their corruption. Allowing presidents to defy congressional impeachment inquiries, aimed at holding presidents accountable for their misconduct, places them beyond the reach of the primary constitutional mechanism—impeachment—designed to check executive tyranny.

A common counter to this argument: What if the forces pushing for impeachment are crassly partisan? Why should a president not be allowed to push back against their cravenness? My answer is that there are multiple constitutional safeguards in place, including the division of authority between the House and Senate, the two-thirds threshold for conviction in the Senate, the Chief Justice's presiding over presidential impeachment trials, and the requirement for senators to be on oath or affirmation throughout the trial.

These are designed to weed out the weak or partisan charges made against presidents. Unless one party has less than a third of the seats in the Senate, presidents are unlikely to be vulnerable to conviction and removal for purely partisan reasons.

Of course, the question can be turned back against itself: What if there are real grounds for considering presidential impeachment but presidents believe they can deflect the matter by complaining that the only justification for impeachment is pure partisanship among the members of Congress pushing for impeachment? The critical thing is not merely to assume that one side is always right (for example, presidents must always win) and the other always wrong. Instead, it makes sense to conduct hearings to put both the case for impeachment and the president's complaints to the test. After all, Nixon had initially complained in opposition to any impeachment inquiry that he had done nothing wrong and that it was driven only by partisanship, but the investigations showed otherwise. While trust is important in our government, no branch has a monopoly over it. As Madison famously said, men are not angels; we must agree with Barbara Jordan, who proclaimed: "My faith in the Constitution is whole; it is complete; it is total."

An additional problem was avoided in Nixon's case. Though the special prosecutor conceded that presidents were likely immune from prosecution at least for as long as they were in office, Nixon asked his Justice Department to examine the question of whether a president may pardon himself. Nixon's lawyers advised that he could because there was no explicit prohibition of it in the Constitution. But three days before Nixon resigned the presidency, the Justice Department determined that a president lacked such power: "Under the fundamental rule that no one may be a judge in his own case," it said, "the President cannot pardon himself."[10] Indeed, it would seem odd, to say the least, that the Constitution allows a president to exercise such power given the shared conviction among the framers and ratifiers that presidents were not above the law. A possible check is, as the Constitution recognizes, that pardons do not preclude impeachments and that presidents who pardoned themselves were abusing their powers and therefore were subject to impeachment. If impeachment is not available as a checking mechanism against such an abuse of power, popularity and elections are the only other checks, which hardly seem to be a match against a lawless president.

Yet another issue came to light several years after Nixon left office. In an interview with David Frost in 1977, Nixon defended his actions in part on the ground "when the president does it . . . that means it is not illegal."[11] The reasoning was that if something is illegal when done by another, it is not illegal if ordered or done by the president, given his position, to act in the public interest, for example, in protecting "national security."

The argument is absurd. The idea that a president is not subject to the same laws as everyone else makes him by definition above the law. If he believes murdering an opponent is justified, he may do that so long as he thinks it is in the public interest; he may break any other law because it conceivably serves his purposes in some way. Of course, presidents attempting to make use of such an argument would declare it is impossible to say presidents broke laws when it is they themselves who have the power (at least in the first example) of determining when laws are broken. The claim is dangerously circular, for there is no apparent outer limit to what a president may do if he is, like a king, always a law unto himself.

Finally, the Supreme Court rendered at least two significant rulings on presidential power in the aftermath of Nixon's presidency. *Nixon v. Fitzgerald*[12] recognized presidents' absolute immunity from civil damages based on their official acts. Subsequent presidents, including Ronald Reagan and Bill Clinton, construed the ruling broadly by arguing that, practically speaking, presidents were on the job 24-7. This construction would recognize as unofficial nearly nothing that a president could do. In the second case, *Nixon v. General Services Administration*,[13] Nixon had pressed the claim that, as a former president, he retained control over documents prepared for him when he was president. The Court rejected that construction. Instead, it recognized that the documents belonged to the government, which controlled whether and where they might be archived. Further, the Court recognized that executive privilege belonged to the office of the president, not to the occupant or to a former occupant. The Court said the interests of former presidents in the documents could be a factor for courts to consider, but that it was hard if not impossible to imagine circumstances in which a former president's interests could trump those of the current occupant because it was the current occupant who was the only official in the position to determine what material could be protected under executive privilege. Former presidents are just that: they no longer wield the powers (or entitlements) of the office any more than former justices have the authority to participate and decide current cases pending before the Supreme Court.

[4]

The Impeachment and Trial of Bill Clinton

President Bill Clinton's impeachment was both surprising and unexpected. More than a century had passed between Andrew Johnson's acquittal and Richard Nixon's resignation, reinforcing the expectation of most Americans that presidential impeachments, however dramatic, were rare constitutional events. Yet when Bill Clinton was inaugurated on January 20, 1993, he was already hated by a good proportion of the electorate and Congress, and he was suspected of all kinds of moral depravity. When the Clintons' friend, Deputy White House Counsel Vince Foster, died by suicide a few months later on July 20, 1993, both Clinton and his wife, Hillary, had many political enemies who suggested they were responsible. Rumors of marital infidelities (and worse) followed Clinton into office, and it did not take long before Clinton found himself on the wrong side of a lawsuit brought by a woman, Paula Jones, who alleged he had sexually harassed her while he was governor of Arkansas. After news of her encounter with Clinton broke in the *American Spectator*, she filed a civil lawsuit for sexual harassment naming Clinton on May 6, 1994.

Both Clintons were repeatedly accused of shady business practices involving a failed real estate development, Whitewater, which made Hillary a lot of money. Throughout the president's first year in office, the Clintons witnessed several former political and business associates prosecuted for criminal misbehavior in the land deal. Before the end of the president's first year in office, he and Hillary had been tipped off about the progress of an investigation run by a Republican lawyer, Jay Stephens, who had been hired by the Resolution Trust Corporation to look into possible criminal activity involved in the Whitewater land deal, and they agreed to turn some documents over to investigators in Stephens's office. In March 1994, the Clintons' longtime friend, and Hillary's former law partner, Webster Hubbell, resigned from his position in the Department of Justice to face criminal charges on another matter. That summer, the House and the Senate Banking Committees opened investigations into the Whitewater affair. On August 5, 1994, a special panel of judges appointed Kenneth Starr, a former federal judge and Solicitor General, as independent counsel charged with investigating the Whitewater matter.

The Jones case and Whitewater plagued Clinton for the remainder of his presidency. Democratic voters and members of Congress had to do contortions to ignore or avoid their implications, one of the more vexing being that Democrats were protecting a serial philanderer while vowing to protect the equality of women in America. Republican voters and members of Congress by and large likened Whitewater to Watergate in every way they could. It was not just to do to the Democrats what they had done to Nixon but to use Watergate as the template for treating nearly every misstep and every suspected misdeed of the Clintons as a new scandal. Indeed, the first major ethics controversy in the Clinton administration, the firing of seven White House travel office personnel in May 1993, was characterized by Clinton critics as "Travelgate." Whitewater and the Paula Jones case were just the two most prominent scandals of the Clinton presidency.

Clinton's personal lawyers managed to delay any discovery in the Jones case until after a Supreme Court decision on whether Clinton, as a sitting president, was entitled to immunity from civil actions based on pre-presidential conduct at least until after he left office. On May 27, 1997, the Supreme Court unanimously authorized the Jones lawsuit to proceed.

The Court gave three reasons for its decision. First, it said that none of its precedents supported Clinton's claim that he was entitled to at least temporary immunity from civil actions based on his unofficial misconduct. It thus rejected there was any precedent for the kind of immunity Clinton was seeking for himself and future presidents.

Second, the Court rejected Clinton's argument that original meaning supported a president's immunity from civil actions based on his unofficial conduct. The Court explained,

[W]e reach the same conclusion about the [relevant] historical materials that Justice [Robert] Jackson described when confronted with an issue concerning the dimensions of the President's power. "Just what our forefathers did envision, or what they would have envisioned had they foreseen modern conditions, must be divined from materials almost as enigmatic as the dreams Joseph was called upon to interpret for

Pharoah. A century and a half of partisan debate and scholarly speculation yields no net result but only supplies more or less apt quotations from respected sources on each side. . . . They largely cancel each other."[1]

Third, the Court rejected Clinton's "strongest argument" that he "occupies a unique office with powers and responsibilities so vast and important that the public demands that he devote his undivided time and attention to his undivided duties."[2] The Court said the unique demands that civil litigation might pose to presidents were vastly overstated. In words that seem naïve in hindsight, the Court put it this way: "[I]n the more than 200-year history of the Republic, only three sitting Presidents have been subjected to lawsuits for their private actions. If the past is any indicator . . . a deluge of such litigation will [not] engulf the presidency. As for the case at hand, if properly managed by the District Court, it appears to us highly unlikely to occupy any substantial amount of [the president's] time."[3] Citing the Watergate tapes case, the Court recognized that it was "settled that the President is subject to judicial process in appropriate circumstances." The Court concluded by placing its faith in the ability of district courts to use their case management authority to take into account the president's unique role in our constitutional system.

Justice Stephen Breyer, a Clinton appointee, wrote a concurrence. He expressed sympathy over the possible burdens civil actions might impose on the president. He also expressed skepticism that about district courts' ability to handle the ramifications civil litigation might pose for presidents' abilities to discharge their unique constitutional duties. He nevertheless agreed that that the president had failed to demonstrate why temporary immunity was needed in this particular case.

The Court had not anticipated Clinton's hubris. Moreover, Clinton, his defenders in Congress, and the media did not foresee how the two proceedings might converge. Clinton made it all possible through his own indiscretions, particularly lies about the relationship he had with a former White House intern and employee of the White House Office of Legislative Affairs, Monica Lewinsky, from 1995 to 1997. Lewinsky had confided the details of her relationship to Linda Tripp, then a coworker in the Department of Defense. Unbeknown to Lewinsky, Tripp recorded their telephone conversations. When Tripp discovered that Lewinsky denied any relationship in an affidavit in the Jones case, she took matters into her own hands. On January 12, 1998, she delivered the tapes of her conversations with Lewinsky to Starr's office, which had already expanded its inquiries into Clinton's misconduct to include not just Whitewater but also the travel office controversy and another controversy that had erupted in 1994 when the head of Clinton's White House Office of Personnel Security gained access to FBI background materials on hundreds of individuals without their permission. Starr's office asked the Attorney General to request an expansion of his investigations to include the Lewinsky matter from the three-judge panel that had authorized his earlier investigations into the Clinton White House. It agreed.

Though Clinton had been reelected in 1996, his legal troubles worsened. He tried unsuccessfully to block his Secret Service detail from testifying about his relationship with Lewinsky based on the novel claim that executive privilege applied to anything they saw or heard while on duty. He failed to prevent testimony from Arkansas state troopers detailed to his office as governor. He failed as well to block White House adviser Bruce Lindsey from testifying on the ground that his communications with Clinton were protected by attorney-client privilege.

Meanwhile, discovery was unfolding in the Jones case. Jones's lawyers, armed with information Tripp had given them, tried to lay a trap for Clinton in his deposition. In trying to avoid the trap, Clinton displayed the same brazenness he had shown when he was having a sexual relationship with Lewinsky. Often, being the smartest guy in the room had worked to Clinton's advantage as a candidate and as president, but this time his cleverness backfired. In written interrogatories, Clinton responded "None" when asked if he had had any sexual relations with Lewinsky. On January 17, Jones's lawyers pressed Clinton in his deposition, where he repeatedly said "No" or "None" in response to questions about whether he had any kind of sexual relationship or affair with Lewinsky. At one point, Clinton testified, "I have never had sexual relations with Monica Lewinsky. I've never had an affair with her."

The Jones lawyers shared the testimony with Starr's Office, which arranged for Clinton to testify before a grand jury. During his testimony, Clinton said, "There's nothing between us" (true at that point since the relationship had ended some time before), but when pressed on whether there was an ongoing relationship, Clinton testified, "It depends on what the meaning of 'is' is. If the—or he—means is and never has been, that is not—that is one thing. If it means there is none, that was a completely true statement." He continued: "Now, if someone had asked me on that day [of the deposition], are you having any kind of sexual relations with Ms. Lewinsky, that is, asked me in a present tense, I would have said no. And it would have been completely true." While no one managed to ask Clinton directly about the details of his relationship with Lewinsky, the repeated image in the media of his dissembling declaration—"It depends on the what the meaning of 'is' is"—hurt his popularity and standing in Congress.

As the charge to seek impeachment picked up steam, Starr's office had to decide what to do with the evidence it had. It had concluded, consistent with the previous actions of the Watergate special prosecutor and policy within the DOJ, that a sitting president was immune to criminal investigation and prosecution. Thus, it determined that Congress was the appropriate authority to address Clinton's misconduct in the first instance. On September 9, Starr's office, with great fanfare, pulled a truck up to the Capitol to unload hundreds of copies of its referral, documenting the details of Clinton's relationship with Lewinsky and 11 impeachable offenses that it told Congress it had "substantial and credible" information to substantiate. The day before the delivery of the Starr Report, the House, under the leadership of Speaker Newt Gingrich, approved an impeachment inquiry against Clinton, which picked up substantial support, especially among Republican House members and voters. On Friday, September 9, two days after the referral had been delivered to Congress, Congress voted overwhelmingly, 363 to 63, to make the report public. More than 100 major newspapers declared Clinton's conduct disgraceful and urged him to resign. Democratic members of Congress overwhelmingly condemned his behavior. Clinton refused to resign.

I

In 1998, for the first time since 1934, the party controlling the White House gained seats in the House of Representatives in the midterm elections. Although Democrats picked up only five seats, their success reduced the Republicans' majority in the House to only 11 seats. The result was such a shock that it led to the resignation of House Speaker Newt Gingrich. For a moment, it looked as if the wind might have come out of the sails of any threatened impeachment of Bill Clinton.

The moment passed, as the lame-duck House, in the final weeks of 1998, intensified its efforts to impeach Clinton. Over the next six weeks, the House moved rapidly to hold hearings and to draft and approve impeachment articles. The first hearing took place less than a week after the midterms. On November 9, 1998, the House Judiciary Committee, for the first time, called constitutional experts to testify in a presidential impeachment proceeding. The panel was unusually large, including 19 witnesses total, with one witness (this book's author) called by both the Republicans and Democrats on the committee and the remainder called by either side.

The hearing helped to frame the constitutional arguments for and against Clinton's impeachment. The main question was whether any of the various charges made against Clinton in the Starr Report, particularly lying under oath and obstruction of justice, were impeachable. Republicans and Democrats relied on many of the same sources, though they interpreted them differently.

Republicans argued that the grounds for impeaching Clinton were straightforward. First, they argued that there was only a single constitutional provision setting forth the grounds for impeachment, which should be applied to—and mean the same thing to—all impeachable offices. Thus, the House's impeachment, conviction, and removal of one judge, Alcee Hastings, for perjury in 1988, and of another judge, Walter Nixon, for lying under oath in 1989, were sound precedents for the House's impeachment of Bill Clinton. Second, they argued that the framers regarded perjury and obstruction of justice as serious matters, reflected further by the fact that federal law made each a felony. Indeed, many argued that Clinton's perjury and obstruction of justice were direct attacks against the integrity of the administration of justice. Third, Republicans pointed out that the House Judiciary Committee had approved an impeachment article against Richard Nixon for obstruction of justice, providing yet another precedent for the House to follow.

Republicans on the House Judiciary Committee repeatedly likened Clinton's misconduct to that of Richard Nixon, who had been charged in the committee's impeachment articles in 1974 with both the "arrogation of power" and "undermining the integrity of the office." Lindsay Graham, then a member of the House and chosen as one of the House Managers, explained, "The day that Richard Nixon failed to answer the subpoena is the day he was subject to impeachment because he took the power from Congress, and he became the judge and jury." Thus, he argued, Clinton's similar refusals to be truthful before the grand jury and to comply with lawful efforts to investigate his relationship with Lewinsky were impeachable. Republicans on the Judiciary Committee (and Republican expert witnesses) further argued that Clinton's perjury and obstruction of justice were direct attacks on the administration of justice, and they stressed the negative impact on military morale if Clinton were let off the hook. Last but hardly least, they argued that Clinton's perjury and obstruction were serious felonies that robbed him of the moral authority as president to remain in charge of enforcing them against everyone else. His oath could not be squared with his constitutional oath "to take care to execute the laws faithfully" and "erode[d] respect for the office of the president." In short, Clinton was no longer fit to be president.

The Democrats in Congress believed that the arguments against impeaching Clinton were even more straightforward. First, they stressed the fact that the Constitution made "other high crimes and misdemeanors" grounds for impeachment, and therefore the misconduct for which presidents may be impeached, convicted, and removed had to be of the same order of seriousness as treason and bribery. They maintained that Clinton's misconduct fell well short of those kinds of serious offenses. As William Van Alstyne suggested in his expert testimony on November 9, Clinton's misconduct was a "low" crime, not the "high" kind required for impeachment. Democrats argued that not all indictable crimes were impeachable, a point backed up in a letter submitted to the House signed by several hundred legal scholars, and that the felonies claimed in this case were not "great" offenses or serious abuses of power, which were examples of impeachable misconduct the framers and ratifiers had cited.

Second, impeachable misconduct required a connection with the president's official duties, and Clinton's lies had no such connection. Thus, Cass Sunstein, then a professor of law at the University of Chicago Law School, argued the Constitution narrowed the scope of impeachable offenses "to allow impeachment for a narrow category of egregious or large-scale abuses of authority that comes from the exercise of distinctly presidential powers." He said: "What is generally necessary [for an impeachable offense] is an egregious abuse of power that the President has by virtue of being President."[4] Sunstein conceded something like murder could be the grounds for impeaching presidents, but otherwise their personal misconduct was inappropriate as a basis for impeachment.[5]

Third, the opponents of Clinton's impeachment argued that presidents should be held to a higher standard than judges in the impeachment process. As the only mechanism for holding judges accountable for their misconduct, impeachment extended to a broader range of their behavior; plus, committing crimes robbed them of the moral and practical authority to oversee trials and even sentence people for the same misconduct. In contrast, presidents were subject to several mechanisms for holding them accountable for misconduct, and the Constitution required a higher, tougher standard for presidential impeachments to ensure that the other mechanisms, such as elections, were viable for lesser and different kinds of misconduct, such as personal peccadilloes. Otherwise, Republicans were using impeachment to overturn a presidential election. Moreover, the different duties of judges and presidents supported treating them differently in the impeachment process. Indeed, the argument was made, misconduct by a judge such as lying under oath had a much more devastating effect on his moral authority to keep doing the job, while it might not have much or any negative effect on a president, whose moral shortcomings were previously known and ratified (twice, in 1992 and 1996) by the American people.

Fourth, Clinton's lawyers and Democrats on the House Judiciary Committee expressed concerns that he was being denied due process, or fundamental fairness. Though the House Judiciary Committee had allowed his impeachment counsel, Greg Craig, to testify against the Starr Report and any unfairness in the process, it denied White House lawyers opportunities to call their own witnesses, present a defense, and cross-examine Republicans' witnesses before the House Judiciary Committee.

Finally, Democratic defenders distinguished Clinton's misconduct from that of Richard Nixon. They pointed out that Nixon's misconduct involved the abuse of his unique presidential powers, such as ordering officials within his administration to harass his political enemies and to cover up his involvement with the Watergate burglary. They also cited the lesson learned from Andrew Johnson's acquittal: the impeachment power should not be used to punish someone because the other side hated the person holding the office.

Several procedural issues also received attention. First, there was a question about the nature of the House's role in impeachment proceedings. Republicans likened it to a grand jury, whose job is to determine whether to charge someone with misconduct. Put another way, the House's job was to decide whether a trial in the Senate was required to conduct further fact-finding and assess the strength of the evidence advanced by either side.

Second, many Democrats insisted that, as a matter of basic fairness, the House should be conducting its own fact-finding and not rely solely on the Starr Report as the factual support for the House's impeachment resolutions. House Republicans, with support from several witnesses, argued that the House was not constitutionally obliged to conduct fact-finding on its own. During my own testimony, I suggested that, while that argument made sense, the House should conduct its own fact-finding to build public confidence in its judgments. The failure to do so reflected partisan haste to impeach Clinton (a president the Republicans plainly hated).

Third, the House Judiciary Committee briefly considered the question of what kind of burden had to be shown to support a judgment from the House to impeach the president.

Most members, all Republican, argued that the burden to impeach was merely a preponderance of the evidence (the lowest burden of proof) and that that burden had been met with the findings set forth in the Starr Report.

A final issue, raised later by Professor Bruce Ackerman of Yale Law School, was that the lame-duck House lacked the constitutional authority to impeach the president. Initially in an op-ed, and then later in a book, Ackerman made two arguments. First, a lame-duck House had no authority to bind the newly constituted House to be sworn in on January 3, 1999. Like other bills, a lame-duck impeachment lapses at the end of the Congress in which it was approved. Thus, the December 19, 1998, impeachment of Clinton should have no legal effect after the newly constituted House came into being in early January 1999.[6] Second, by shortening the transition period between Election Day and the days on which a newly constituted Congress or a new president was sworn in, the Twentieth Amendment made any consequential decisions made by a lame-duck House or Senate unconstitutional. They should instead be made by the newly constituted Congress, especially because there was plenty of time to allow that to happen.

It was an interesting argument that had no sway in either chamber. The prevailing thinking was that an impeachment done by the House was a completed constitutional action, one that necessarily passed to the Senate for subsequent action. The lapsing of a bill was a consequence of House or Senate rules. Nothing in the text of the Constitution barred a lame-duck House from approving impeachment articles.

Bills lapsed because the rules said so, but they said nothing about impeachments lapsing. Once approved by the House, impeachment articles—under the rules—were transmitted to the Senate, regardless of the time of year or legislative session.

On December 19, the House rendered its judgment: a majority, entirely Republican members, approved two impeachment articles against Bill Clinton, one charging him with lying under oath to the grand jury (228–206) and the other with obstruction of justice (221–212). The House did not approve two other proposed articles, which the committee had approved, one charging Clinton with having lied in the Paula Jones case and the other charging him with abuse of power (supposedly by using the powers of the presidency to thwart the investigation into his relationship with Lewinsky).

II

Senate leaders wasted no time preparing for the first presidential impeachment trial in more than a century. Senate Majority Leader Trent Lott worked with Minority Leader Tom Daschle to work out procedures for the trial. They used the rules fashioned for Johnson's trial as a template, but knowing that there were not the votes in the Senate to convict and remove Clinton, they developed what they regarded as a fair but efficient way to conduct the trial so as to fulfill the Senate's constitutional responsibilities. On January 8, 1999, the Senate, meeting in its old chamber for the first time since 1859, unanimously approved the procedures, which included a two-week trial, agreements to allow each side to call three witnesses who would be deposed off-site, and requirements that senators attend all sessions but not be allowed to talk to each other during the proceedings. The Chief Justice would preside, read questions from senators to the House Managers or Clinton's counsel, and be allowed to make rulings, which could be overruled by a majority of the Senate.

Some preliminary procedural matters were quickly resolved. Several senators, along with reporters and experts, wondered whether the Senate should adopt a uniform burden of proof and rules of evidence. These matters had come up before, particularly during three judicial impeachments in the late 1980s, at which time the Senate voted not to adopt either of these. While those judgments were not binding on the Senate, senators agreed to the same outcomes for the Clinton trial. It was widely accepted that senators were each entitled to choose whichever burden of proof they deemed appropriate and that evidentiary rules were not needed.

The trial began on January 7, 1999, and ended on February 9. There were no fireworks and no surprises. The House Managers, led by Jim Sensenbrenner of Wisconsin, marshaled the evidence, in the Starr Report and from the few witnesses deposed for the Senate, to buttress their arguments that Clinton had lied under oath and obstructed justice, and that these misdeeds were impeachable. Clinton's lawyers, led by Chief White House Counsel Charles Ruff, ripped into the Starr Report as one-sided and done without any input from or participation by Clinton's lawyers, and reiterated that his misconduct was personal and trivial and had no connection to his duties.

Prior to the final vote in the trial, the Senate faced three procedural issues. The first involved the question of whether the Senate had the authority to issue findings of fact as to Clinton's guilt in a vote separate from one on whether he should be convicted, removed, and disqualified. The proponents argued that nothing in the Constitution expressly barred a vote on the underlying facts in a trial; and there was arguably some precedent, in the form of Senate practice before 1936, to take separate votes on impeached officials' guilt and on removal. The critics made two arguments. First, they argued that impeachment was the exclusive means for Congress to hold presidents accountable for misconduct. Indeed, they said, the only reason that Republicans were pushing for such separate votes was to allow them to declare Clinton guilty in the absence of conviction and removal.

Second, they argued that a vote on findings of fact was tantamount to an unconstitutional bill of attainder, in which the legislature (here Congress) imposed punishment on someone in the absence of a judicial proceeding. Proponents said the measure was not a bill of attainder, since it had no tangible effect. When Democrats united in opposition to the proposed finding of fact, Republicans dropped the proposal because it was clear they did not have the votes.

The final procedural issue was whether the Senate should allow its final deliberations to be held in open session. The Senate rules required that they be held in closed session and that modifying any rule required two-thirds approval by the Senate. The Senate's vote of 59 to 41 to hold Senate deliberation in public fell short of that threshold.

For many senators, the final vote did not come fast enough. On February 9, neither impeachment article received support from much more than half the Senate, and therefore each fell well short of the two-thirds threshold for conviction and removal. The vote on the first impeachment article was strictly along party lines, with all 55 Republicans voting in favor but all 45 Democrats opposing. Five Republican senators crossed the aisle to join their Democratic colleagues in voting against the second article. No Democrat voted to convict Clinton.

Throughout the trial, Chief Justice William Rehnquist took great pains to maintain a low profile. He had no interest in repeating any of Chase's earlier mistakes and becoming the center of attention. The only notable ruling he made was to agree with a motion made by Senator Tom Harkin that had objected to the House Managers' repeated reference to the senators as "jurors." Rehnquist agreed: "The Senate is not simply a jury. It is a court in this case." He later described his experience by paraphrasing a favorite quote of his from a comic opera written by Gilbert and Sullivan: "I did nothing in particular, and I did it very well."

There was little cause for celebration among the Democrats (though there had been a pep rally at the White House after the House voted to impeach Clinton). The episode did permanent damage to Clinton's legacy, as he had become only the second American president impeached by the House and tried in the Senate. The episode strained the already fraught relationship between Clinton and Vice President Al Gore, as Clinton's morally dubious conduct haunted Gore throughout his own run for the presidency the next year. Clinton's impeachment and trial left him without the political capital to do anything significant during the remainder of his presidency. (A friend of the author's working in the administration remarked at the time that Clinton had "miniaturized the presidency.") Numerous reports suggested Hillary made it clear that Clinton owed her, and she put him to work on building her own political identity and career.

The trial ended with a historic first when the vast majority of senators issued formal explanations for their votes. Nearly every one of the 72 senators who issued explanations condemned Clinton's misconduct. Even Democrats who had voted against Clinton's conviction expressed their disgust for his misconduct, for which Clinton never apologized in public (or acknowledged as misconduct).

Of the 72 senators who issued public statements after the trial, there were 34 Democrats, all of whom had voted not to convict Clinton; four of the five Republicans who had voted against both impeachment articles and conviction on the second impeachment article; and three of the five Republicans who had voted to convict on the first but not the second article of impeachment. Of the 38 senators who published statements on their reasons for voting not to convict on the basis of either article, more than half (27) explained they had done so because they believed the misconduct cited as the basis for both articles did not rise to the level of impeachable offenses. Sixteen of the 38, all Democrats, explained that the overzealousness of the House Managers and House leadership influenced their votes, while 15 Democrats and Republican Senator Arlen Specter said that the House Managers had not proven the misconduct alleged in either impeachment article. Two Republican senators said they had voted not to convict Clinton on the first article even though they believed the House Managers had proven all the charges they had made against Clinton. Fred Thompson, a Republican senator from Tennessee, said that he had voted to convict only on the basis of the second impeachment article because he regarded the first as having been framed too vaguely and without specifying the particular statements Clinton made that were perjurious. It stands to reason that the senators who voted to convict Clinton on the bases of both articles believed that he had committed impeachable offenses.

III

Clinton's impeachment and trial raised several significant constitutional concerns and consequences. The first involved the ramifications of the fact that both he and Nixon—the two most recent presidents to face impeachment—were impeached and tried in their second terms. For all the talk about how the impeachment process should not substitute for elections, elections were no longer options to address their misconduct. When the Twenty-Second Amendment had been ratified to preclude presidents from serving more than two terms, it removed one of the checks against presidential misconduct and, as a result, made impeachment even more important for dealing with presidential misbehavior, whether it was before elections, during the first term, or at some point in the second term. If censure was not a viable option for addressing presidential misconduct, even more pressure was placed on impeachment to be an effective mechanism to check presidential misconduct.

But the Clinton acquittal underscored the ineffectiveness of impeachment. Clinton's popularity steadily rose during his impeachment ordeal, topping 70% public approval at the time of his acquittal. If an unpopular president like Johnson and a popular president like Clinton could not be convicted for misconduct, impeachment hardly inspired confidence. Of course, a major reason was the two-thirds threshold for conviction in the Senate, a threshold that seemed impossible to meet if the senators from the president's party united—as Democrats did—in opposition to conviction. Without impeachment as a viable means for addressing presidents' serious abuses of power, the presidency itself became more powerful and unaccountable in the wake of Clinton's acquittal.

A second major issue raised by the Clinton impeachment and trial was the role of the media in handling or addressing presidential misconduct. With Nixon, it was the media, including the reporting of Woodward and Bernstein and the televised hearings, that helped to bring Nixon down. Yet with Clinton, the opposite seemed to happen. The 24-7 news cycle gave proponents and opponents of his impeachment ample opportunities to plead their cases to their bases. It facilitated the hardening of positions, not educating people about the process. Indeed, the rise of infotainment, or soft news (commentary and speculation rather than hard data), was just beginning at the time of Clinton's impeachment but fueled increasingly partisan and extreme rhetoric about the cases for and against his impeachment and conviction.

This second issue was linked to another. While it took nearly two years of congressional investigations to uncover the "smoking gun" that hastened the end of the Nixon presidency, the Clinton proceedings took six months from start to finish. Yet for the American public and Congress, that seemed too long. The proliferation of media outlets made people more impatient to fast-forward to the results. Indeed, it seems impossible to imagine that, after the Clinton trial, the American public or Congress would have the patience to conduct investigations that last anywhere close to two years. That development could not be good for the future of holding presidents accountable for their misconduct, since proceedings would be unlikely to have the time to build popular support or would risk being done too hastily to satisfy the public hunger for a swift outcome.

A third consequence of Clinton's acquittal was that it obscured the scope of impeachable offenses. If neither Johnson (by violating the Tenure in Office Act) nor Clinton (by the perjury he was later found guilty of by a federal judge) committed any impeachable offenses, a major question was left for another day: What kinds of abuses of power would qualify as the grounds for impeachment and conviction?

In addition, the Clinton case highlighted a peculiar consequence of a lame-duck House's impeachment of a president (or any other official, for that matter). Several House members who voted on Clinton's impeachment had been elected to the Senate in the midterm elections of 1998, and they were allowed to vote as senators on the very same matter. That outcome struck many people as unfair, and it was certainly odd. Yet the Senate handled the matter the same way it handled the applicable burdens of proof and rules of evidence: by having each new senator make the determination for himself or herself on whether to forego voting on conviction and removal after having voted on the question of impeachment in the House.

These problems overshadowed one of the most important aspects of the Clinton impeachment. When all was said and done, polling indicated that 76% of the American people believed that the case against Clinton involved purely personal misconduct that should not have been made the basis for impeachment. It appeared as if the public not only tracked the proceedings but also understood the core issues. While members of Congress were under no constitutional compulsion to take polling into account, members of Congress ignored the public sentiment at their own risk.

The First Impeachment and Trial
of Donald Trump

When Donald Trump declared during the 2016 presidential election "I could stand in the middle of Fifth Avenue and shoot somebody, and I wouldn't lose any voters," few people thought he was kidding. By the time the threat to impeach him became serious in the fall of 2019, he had been investigated by a special counsel and was under investigations by the Attorney General of the State of New York, the Manhattan District Attorney, and Congress. Yet throughout it all, he maintained firm control over the Republican Party, including members in Congress and voters. It was hard to imagine what he could do to lose their ardent support.

In the end, it was not Trump's self-dealing, or his numerous lies to the public, or his defiance of Congress that put him squarely in the crosshairs of impeachment. As had happened with both Andrew Johnson and Bill Clinton, it was his own conduct that got him in trouble. He gave the Democratic majority in the House little choice but to impeach.

The matter, triggering the vote, came to light from people working within his own administration. During a phone conversation with the newly elected president of Ukraine, Volodymyr Zelensky, whose country was battling invasion from Russian forces, President Trump said he wished "to ask a favor" from Zelensky, specifically his agreement to announce criminal investigations into (1) Hunter Biden and his father, Joe Biden, whom Trump expected to be a major opponent in the next year's presidential election; and (2) a discredited theory that Ukraine, not Russia, attempted to interfere with the 2016 presidential election. Trump delayed releasing funds, presumably expecting that Zelensky's agreement to the "favor" requested by Trump as as a possible condition for granting Zelensky's request to visit the White House and releasing military assistance to Ukraine. Eventually, the president allowed the money appropriated for Ukraine to be released, but in the aftermath of a whistleblower's reporting Trump's request to the inspector general for the intelligence community, Trump, Republicans in the House, and later some Republican senators pressed for the whistleblower to be investigated and for his name to be made public. Trump pressed administration officials not to speak with congressional investigators and to agree publicly with his repeated pronouncement that the call "was perfect." At the end of October 2019, the House approved an impeachment inquiry, voting 232 to 196, almost entirely along party lines.

I

Even before the House Intelligence Committee completed its investigations into the Zelensky matter began, and before the House Judiciary Committee began its impeachment hearings in earnest, President Trump, his White House counsel, and several Republican supporters in the House trashed Speaker Nancy Pelosi, House Democrats, and the case for impeachment in hyperbolic rants, which made little to no sense as legal or constitutional arguments. But that was not their objective; they were making appeals to energize Trump's base and to confuse or distract the American people. They proclaimed House Democrats were on a "witch-hunt," that the president was the most persecuted leader in American history, that the impeachment effort was "partisan," that any witnesses against Trump were "never Trumpers" even if they had supported him or served in previous Republican administrations; they called any charges of misconduct "unfounded" and based on "hearsay," called the proceedings "unfair," and declared that the proceedings were not consistent with the "bipartisan precedent" on presidential impeachment.[1]

Much of the rhetoric was bluster or simply unfounded (for example, there was no "bipartisan precedent" on impeachment that bound the House in any way) and not worth dignifying with responses. Yet demonstrating the problems with just one of the common refrains hopefully sets the record on impeachment a little straighter: the idea that the impeachment of Trump was "partisan" was nonsense as a legal argument, though it made some political sense by demonizing the opposition. Just because a bill may have been approved by majorities of only Republicans in the House and the Senate, and later signed by a Republican president, does not make that bill any less of a constitutional enactment than if it had differently constituted support. There is no such thing as a "partisan" bill. As far as the Constitution is concerned, there are just bills, which are either approved in compliance with the constitutional requirements for lawmaking or not. The Constitution does not require a certain kind of composition of the members voting for a bill—or for an impeachment—to make it lawful. All that matters is whether there is a majority in each chamber to approve the bill, and the party of the president is irrelevant to whether or not the bill is constitutional. The composition of the majorities that enact legislation or approve impeachment resolutions is irrelevant to their lawfulness. The claim was no better than arguing that the House's actions were unlawful because they occurred on a certain day of the week.

But lurking not so far beneath the surface of the arguments of the president and his counsel was something dangerous: the positions and arguments Trump and his defenders took during the impeachment were consistent with a theory of executive power not yet endorsed by the Court (or by most legal scholars or Congress). This was the unitary theory of the executive, first championed in 1988 by the late Justice Antonin Scalia in a dissent (joined by no one else) that posited that the president should be in complete control over the exercise of all executive power and therefore all people exercising executive power.[2] When Trump asserted that he did not have to comply with a legislative subpoena seeking information produced within the executive branch, he was implicitly arguing he had an absolute executive privilege. The unitary theory was undoubtedly what the president was referring to when he said during his first term that the Constitution gave him as president "the right to do whatever I want." His subsequent lack of cooperation with the impeachment inquiry, refusal to comply with subpoenas from the House

Judiciary and Intelligence Committees, claims of absolute executive privilege allowing him to refuse to share information (even about illegal activity within the White House), along with other authorities and assertions of absolute immunity from criminal investigation and prosecution can all be traced to the unitary theory of the executive. Ironically, as Trump took great pains to demonstrate in the remainder of his presidency, it served another purpose entirely: placing the president beyond the reach of Congress or prosecution for breaking the law. Trump maintained that his reelection was the only legitimate venue for holding him accountable, even for misconduct undermining that election. In other words, the unitary theory of the executive, in its most robust form, treats the president as above the law.

II

The president's arguments against impeachment did not just extend throughout the House's impeachment proceedings. The more his claims were pressed in the media and Congress, the more they framed Republicans' responses. They framed and fueled the arguments Republicans made in the House and Senate against impeachment, and thus Republicans defending Trump found themselves expressing nothing more than talking points and political hyperbole. When Democrats responded with evidence or cogent arguments made on the basis of constitutional history or prior precedents in the impeachment process, Republicans answered with political claptrap and personal insults. For example, when two of the three constitutional experts called by Democrats, one from Harvard Law School and the other from Stanford, testified before the House Judiciary Committee on the grounds for impeaching Trump, Louis Gohmert, a Republican congressman from Texas, responded, "If you love America, mamas, don't let your babies grow up to go to Harvard or Stanford Law School."[3] Similarly, another Republican member of the House Judiciary Committee, Matt Gaetz of Florida, answered cogent arguments made by Democratic witnesses on the law of presidential impeachment by asking them whether they had voted for Trump and accusing them of political bias because they had donated money to President Barack Obama's campaign. If there were any serious arguments based on the Constitution, they were obscured by the antics of Republican congressmen who opposed Trump's impeachment.

In November, congressional hearings and Republican antics revved up. Led by Adam Schiff, Democrat of California, the House Intelligence Committee initiated an investigation in November. The committee called seventeen witnesses to testify behind closed doors on Trump's conversation with Zelensky and subsequent actions, but more than a dozen officials from Trump inner's circle ignored subpoenas to testify to the committee. Despite repeated attempts by Republican members of the House, including several House Intelligence Committee members, to stop the closed-door interviews, claiming that they should be held in public, Schiff's committee completed its investigation and released its report on December 3, 2019.

The House Judiciary Committee, chaired by Jerrold Nadler of New York, used the House Intelligence Committee's report as the factual foundation for its hearings on the grounds for impeaching President Trump. To expedite the matter, Nadler scheduled only two panels to appear before his committee. Throughout these proceedings, Republicans on the Committee engaged in a series of procedural motions intended to slow down, if not stifle, the impeachment of the president.

The first hearing was a panel of four constitutional experts who testified on December 4, 2019. Three witnesses were called by committee Democrats (including this book's author), and one witness was called by Republican committee members. Their testimony provided the most extensive discussion on the grounds for impeaching President Trump in the House in 2019.

First, all four scholars agreed that impeachable offenses were not limited to, or required to be, indictable offenses. They quoted extensively from the framers and ratifiers in support of this proposition. For example, in *The Federalist Papers*, Hamilton explained: "The President of the United States would be liable to be impeached, tried, and, upon conviction of treason, bribery, or other high crimes or misdemeanors, removed from office; and would afterward be liable to prosecution and punishment in the ordinary course of law," in direct contrast with "the king of Great Britain," for whom "there is no constitutional tribunal to which he is amendable; no punishment to which he can be subjected without involving the crisis of national revolution." During the constitutional convention, George Mason of Virginia wondered, "Shall any man be above Justice? Above all shall that man be above it, who can commit the most extensive injustice?" He asked rhetorically: "Shall the man who has practiced corruption & by that means procured his appointment in the first instance, be suffered to escape punishment?" James Madison expressed concern that a president might "pervert his administration into a scheme of peculation or oppression" or "betray his trust to foreign leaders." Edmond Randolph of Virginia worried that the "executive will have great opportunit[ies] of abusing his power; particularly in time of war when military force, and in some respects the public money will be in his hands." William Davie, a North Carolina delegate, warned: "If he be not impeachable whilst in office, he will spare no effort or means whatever to get himself re-elected."[4]

Second, the three scholars called by the Democrats argued that the House did not have to wait, as several Republican committee members had urged, for the completion of litigation over the legitimacy of its subpoenas to Trump and other administration officials before drafting impeachment articles charging Trump with his failure to comply. They stressed that the Constitution's vesting the House with the "sole power of impeachment" meant that the House did not have to wait for the courts to legitimize its procedures or to give it a green light before it would be allowed to proceed with drafting impeachment articles against Trump. The House had "sole" discretion over the rules for its proceedings and the grounds for impeaching the president.

Third, the three scholars argued that the evidence set forth in the House Intelligence Committee's report revealed that the president committed several impeachable offenses. Among these were bribery (Stanford Professor Pam Karlan described the common law of bribery before and after the ratification of the Constitution as penalizing "when you took private benefits, or asked for private benefits, in return for an official act"[5]), extortion, obstruction of Congress, and obstruction of justice.

Trump's defenders and the one Republican witness on impeachment made several counterclaims. First, they dismissed the impeachment attempt as partisan, unfair, and a rush to judgment. They said there was not yet enough evidence to prove Trump did something wrong, ignoring the irony that he was preventing its disclosure to Congress. They said the hearings were merely the latest effort to oust Trump, which had begun immediately after he was elected president in 2016. Thus, they said, the House was trying to undo that election. There was more than a little madness to the Republicans' arguments. They were hardly alone in recognizing that there was no possibility of securing a conviction in the Senate, where Republicans held a majority of seats. Thus, Republican House members repeatedly reminded voters that the House's intelligence and impeachment hearings were a waste of time and effort and that the House should be spending its time on matters of greater concern among the electorate.

Second, they defended Trump's conduct as unimpeachable, though the Republican witness, Jonathan Turley of George Washington University Law School, conceded that impeachable offenses did not have to be indictable crimes (an assertion he made when testifying in the Clinton impeachment proceedings). Nonetheless, Turley insisted that "the record" did not show Trump had done anything impeachable, though again he conceded that, if Democrats could prove what they claimed, Trump had engaged in impeachable misconduct.

The second hearing convened by Chairman Nadler featured two witnesses who had testified before the House Intelligence Committee. Among the concerns expressed during their testimony were the president's threats to punish people who testified against him and public statements vilifying a former United States ambassador to Ukraine, Marie Yovanovitch, while she was testifying before the House Intelligence Committee in November.

On December 10, the House Judiciary Committee publicized the two articles of impeachment it had drafted against Trump. The first charged that his defiance of at least 10 subpoenas (and ordering cabinet secretaries and others to ignore them) obstructed Congress's lawful investigations into his misconduct. The second article charged abuse of power, including conditioning congressionally appropriated funds on a foreign leader's cooperation to help his reelection. On December 13, the House Judiciary Committee approved the articles strictly along party lines. Again along party lines, the House on December 18, 2019, approved the first article of impeachment (230–197) and the second article (229–198). On the first article, two Democratic House members voted against impeaching Trump (and a third voted "present"), while one (formerly) Republican member of the House voted to impeach him. All Republican House members voted against the second impeachment article, while three Democrats voted against it (and another voted "present").

The House did not forward the impeachment articles immediately to the Senate. Speaker Nancy Pelosi held them for several weeks in the hope of getting Senate Majority Leader Mitch McConnell of Kentucky to agree to call witnesses and not to engage in a cover-up of Trump's misconduct. McConnell never agreed (nor did he have to, at least as a constitutional matter), and on January 15, 2020, after the Senate received the two articles of impeachment, McConnell declared: "I'm confident that this body can rise above short-termism and factional fever[] and serve the long-term best interests of our nation."[6]

III

Chief Justice John Roberts captured the dynamic within Donald Trump's first Senate impeachment trial, which began on January 16, 2020, when, near the end of the day, he "admonish[ed] both the House Managers and the president's counsel in equal terms to remember that they are addressing the world's greatest deliberative body. One reason it has earned that title is because its members avoid speaking in a manner and using language that is not conducive to civil discourse." Not much improved after that, with infighting among the House Managers (led by Congressman Schiff), more vitriol from White House lawyers, and several Republican senators' disregard for Senate rules. Otherwise, Chief Justice Roberts, like Chief Justice Rehnquist (for whom he had clerked) in the Clinton trial, rarely interjected himself into the proceedings and avoided making rulings (though he declined to answer a question posed by Senator Rand Paul, which angered Paul). Roberts largely ignored senators' conduct: milling around and conversing in the back of the Senate chamber, doodling or reading material not related to the trial, and exchanging notes on the Senate floor.

Even at the start of the trial, the two sides found little if any common ground. Unlike then–Majority Leader Lott and then–Minority Leader Daschle in Clinton's Senate impeachment trial, the Majority Leader McConnell and Minority Leader Chuck Schumer of New York could agree only on a skeletal framework for the Senate proceedings that pointedly did not include any commitments on witnesses.

Before the Senate, White House lawyers and counsel for Trump made three basic arguments. The first was that Trump's conduct had to be criminal to be impeachable, but the House Managers had not shown any such thing. In an unusual turn, Trump had Alan Dershowitz, an old friend and retired Harvard law professor, make an appearance on his behalf at the trial. During the Clinton impeachment proceedings, Dershowitz had publicly opposed Clinton's impeachment, arguing that "you don't need a technical crime" to serve as the basis for impeachment but that Clinton had not engaged in the kind of serious offenses meriting conviction and removal. Standing before the Senate in 2020, Dershowitz argued that impeachment, in fact, required proof of "a crime or criminal behavior." He declared that "abuse of power and obstruction of Congress" were not sufficiently criminal in nature to qualify as impeachable offenses. He explained away the perceived discrepancies in his comments between 1998 and 2020 on the ground that he had relied on "academic consensus" rather than research to answer the question of what qualifies as impeachable misconduct in the Clinton proceedings but had found, after doing his own research, that criminality was an essential element of an impeachable offense. Dershowitz went even further in response to a question from Republican Senator Ted Cruz of Texas, arguing that "if a president does something he believes will help him get elected in the public interest, that cannot be the kind of quid pro quo that results in impeachment." When CNN commentators, including Jeffrey Toobin, ridiculed Dershowitz's argument as nonsensical and tantamount to licensing tyranny, he blamed CNN for inaccurately editing his comments and sued the network for defamation.[7]

The second argument against Trump's impeachment was that the proceedings against him in the House were constitutionally unfair because Trump was not allowed to call witnesses, present evidence, exclude evidence as hearsay, and cross-examine Democrats' witnesses. The argument appealed to Trump voters, but it was not true. The House Judiciary Committee had allowed Trump's lawyers to cross-examine witnesses and make their case, but they chose not to do so. They also had the chance to present witnesses before the Senate but chose instead to threaten Democrats that they would call Joe and Hunter Biden if Democrats attempted to call any witnesses of their own. Republicans in the Senate, parroting the president, repeatedly claimed that the hearings ought to focus on the fact that Hunter Biden had benefited enormously from massive fraud and that Joe Biden, as vice president, had pushed for the removal of a prosecutor supposedly looking into Hunter Biden's fraud. In fact, Biden was following American foreign policy in urging removal of the Ukrainian prosecutor because the prosecutor was not tough on corruption

Trump's lawyers made several other arguments, which also played fast and loose with the facts and law. Deputy White House Counsel Pat Philbin argued House Managers had failed to show Trump had any "illicit motive," insisted there was no proof Trump did anything wrong, and alleged House Managers had produced nothing but unsubstantiated hearsay. The claim that there was no proof of Trump's misconduct, or culpability, required ignoring the testimony of witnesses under oath who had been on more than one call with Trump and were reporting directly on what they had witnessed and heard.

Moreover, Trump attorney Jay Sekulow argued that an investigation opened in 2016 into possible ties between the Trump campaign and Russia had investigated Trump personally, though it did not. When the Justice Department opened an investigation into Trump personally, it was because of his firing of Jim Comey as FBI director. Pam Bondi, another Trump lawyer, spent most her time informing the Senate about the corruption of the Bidens, though the Republican-led Senate Foreign Relations Committee later found no credible evidence supporting the accusations.

On January 29 and 30, lawyers on both sides answered questions that senators had written down on cards for the

Chief Justice to ask. The questions largely tracked senators' party affiliations, with Democratic senators tossing softballs to the House Managers and with Republican senators doing the same for Trump's lawyers. Alaska Senator Lisa Murkowski and Tennessee Senator Lamar Alexander, both Republicans, asked Trump's lawyers if his withholding aid from Ukraine was impeachable. They answered that it was not. But when three Democratic senators asked both sides who was paying Rudy Giuliani, who had gone to Ukraine to find dirt on the Bidens, Congressman Schiff said he did not know, while Trump attorney Sekulow declared it irrelevant. Trump publicly denied asking Giuliani to do any such thing.

At the end of January, in the only genuinely dramatic episode in the trial, the Senate voted 51 to 49 not to call any witnesses. Two Republicans joined all 45 Democrats and two Independents to vote for witnesses, particularly former National Security Advisor John Bolton, who had served under Trump and written a book detailing Trump's freezing aid to Ukraine and asking Zelensky to meet with Giuliani to discuss the Bidens. Trump, who had fired Bolton, said the book was filled with lies. Trump's Justice Department tried in vain to block the book's release to ensure that it contained no confidential or privileged information.

The Senate's vote against calling witnesses foreshadowed the acquittal. One day before the final Senate vote, Trump delivered a triumphant State of the Union Address, which ended with Speaker Pelosi ripping his speech in half. The next day, February 5, the Senate voted 52 to 48 to acquit Trump on the first impeachment article. One Republican senator, Mitt

Romney, crossed party lines to vote guilty and thereby made history as the first senator to vote to convict a president of his own party. Strictly along party lines, the Senate voted 53 to 47 not to convict Trump for obstructing Congress. The two votes were the lowest numbers yet of senators' voting to convict in a presidential impeachment trial.

Fewer senators released public statements after the trial compared to after Clinton's trial, though several granted interviews to explain their votes. Maine's Susan Collins said she had voted to acquit because "I believe that the president has learned from this case." When Trump publicly scoffed at her statement, reiterated his actions were perfect, and vowed to get even with administration and other officials who had been disloyal, she corrected her statement from "believe" to "hope."

IV

Among the many ramifications of Trump's first acquittal, several were important for impeachment. First, Trump was now the third president impeached by the House but acquitted in the Senate. Never breaking 50% in approval ratings, it was not Trump's popularity within the country that secured the outcome. Indeed, polling immediately after the acquittal indicated that, while 46% of the American people believed he had committed impeachable offenses, 28% said Trump did something wrong but not impeachable, and 25% said they believed he had done nothing wrong. Trump's solid control of Republicans in the House and Senate ensured his acquittal, and his acquittal demonstrated again the relative ineffectiveness of impeachment as a mechanism to address presidential miscon-duct. For the second time in a row, the unity of the president's party in opposition to impeachment ensured the Senate never came close to convicting the president. The threshold for con-viction proved yet again too high for any practical possibility of convicting a miscreant president.

Second, Trump's acquittal damaged or even squashed the utility of impeachment as a means for forcing presidents to resign rather than endure impeachment inquiries and hear-ings. Trump said a "big difference" between him and Nixon was that "Nixon left. I don't leave." Though acknowledging the Watergate scandal as a "dark period" in American history, Trump aligned himself with Nixon's nostrum that something was not illegal if done by the president. For many, Trump's acquittal revived the imperial presidency, which Nixon's downfall had cut short.

Most senators did not agree, however, that Trump's phone call with Zelensky was "perfect" or that his actions in freez-ing aide and attempting to leverage Zelensky into doing as Trump asked were perfectly appropriate. For instance, Ten-nessee's Lamar Alexander conceded Trump did something wrong but said the upcoming presidential election was the proper venue for handling that. John Thune, part of the Re-publican leadership team in the Senate, said the same thing. Adding those and other voices to the Democrats' condemna-tion of Trump left an indelible mark on his presidency, even if the Senate fell well short of conviction.

Third, revelations after Trump's acquittal illustrated the dangers of Trump's conception of presidential power. Within

48 hours of his acquittal, Trump announced the beginning of a purge of people in his administration not completely loyal to him and sacked his ambassador to the European Union; he also had a security detail march Colonel Alexander Vindman, a former aide to the National Security Council who had testified against him, out of the White House. Trump railed against the people who had criticized him as "crooked" and "evil," and his press secretary declared that those who had testified against him "should pay for" their disloyalty.[8] In April, Trump fired the inspector general who had received the whistleblower report and shared it with appropriate officials in the administration; Trump found insubordinate his failure to come directly to him with the report. There was more fallout to come. The night after the acquittal vote, DOJ and the Office of Management and Budget acknowledged that some of the emails that Trump had refused to share with Congress revealed details about why military aid to Ukraine had been frozen. Trump boasted that he had all the information Congress had wanted but had kept it to himself because he could. And when Trump announced in October, just as the impeachment inquiry was heating up, that he was pulling American troops out of northern Iran at the request of Turkey's president, Tayyip Erdogan, he turned a blind eye to the massacre of America's Kurdish allies that ensued. While there were rumors that Trump had cut the deal to help his investments in Turkey, no such evidence was ever forthcoming, consistent with Trump's determination to keep much of his activity as president hidden from public and congressional review.

Yet another possible casualty of Trump's first impeachment was the toll it had taken on facts as pertinent to the search for truth or holding public officials accountable for misconduct. Less than a week after Trump's inauguration, his adviser Kellyanne Conway (who had led his first campaign) responded to a question about Trump's press secretary inflating the number of people who attended the swearing-in ceremony saying there were "alternative facts" in support. "Alternative facts" were lies, but Trump, throughout his first term and certainly during his first impeachment, relished proclaiming alternative facts for nearly every unfounded claim—or lie—he uttered. During the first impeachment trial, Trump had publicly said that he did not know what Giuliani was doing and that Giuliani was not working for him. After the trial, Trump said Giuliani was in Ukraine at his request to uncover dirt on the Bidens. His acquittal seemed to reward that misbehavior, and for the remainder of 2020, Trump and his reelection campaign increasingly used alternative facts to downplay or deny the devastating effects of the COVID-19 pandemic and to paint their own version of events, including impeachment.

The problem was not just voters' willingness to believe what they wanted to believe, for that had always been a feature of the electoral process. The dangers were in the erosion of the rule of law resulting from Trump's defiance of subpoenas and of the lawful authority of Congress; faith in factual evidence was no more. Law is an evidence-based profession, relying on the adjudicative process to verify factual claims, but Trump's lawyers showed no apparent concern for the truth; instead they looked to protect Trump's "truth." Their presentations in the trial were designed almost entirely to appeal to an audience of one: the president who had hired them. Evidence revealed during and after the proceedings indicated that lawyers within the administration had helped to hide or destroy damaging documents.

The fifth ramification of Trump's trial is that it left the next presidential election as the only venue where Trump allowed he could be held accountable. Having been acquitted for asking Zelensky to help his reelection, Trump was motivated to ask other foreign leaders for help. Indeed, before impeachment proceedings began in 2019 he answered a reporter who asked if he would accept foreign help in the 2020 election: "I think I'd take it." He moved quickly in response to pressure from his aides to downplay the remark as a "mistake," but he distinguished dirt from a foreign agent from the conversations and interactions he had with foreign leaders. When asked by George Stephanopoulos if he would call the FBI if Russia, China, or any other foreign entity offered negative information about his opponent, Trump said, "I think maybe, you do both. I think you might want to listen. There's nothing wrong with listening." In other public statements, he stressed he had never reported anything to the FBI.

The November 2020 election was all that stood between Trump and another four years, which he vowed to use to even the score with political enemies. Indeed, Trump's supporters had warned that the impeachment effort would backfire against Democrats in the upcoming presidential election, but concerns about Trump's impeachment or acquittal had largely faded by that time. For the remainder of 2020, it was not impeachment or its fallout that dominated the news or the public's interest but instead the spread of a pandemic that, by Election Day, had claimed the lives of more than 300,000 Americans. Trump downplayed and lied about the virus, including repeated pronouncements that the numbers "are looking MUCH better, going down almost everywhere."[9] The truth was just the opposite. Yet when the votes were finally counted (and of course I mean the legal votes), the outcome was not much different than the one in 2016. The parity of the parties, in terms of their relative strengths around the country, remained largely the same; party loyalty remained nearly as strong as it had been in the past; and concerns about cultural issues continued to divide Americans, but they were shifting to topics like personal autonomy and social issues rather than economic regulations and class warfare. The shifts were slight, but they were big enough that Trump lost in the general election to Joe Biden, who won the exact same number of Electoral College votes in 2020 that President Trump had won in 2016. Trump did not blame the impeachment or the pandemic but widespread voter fraud as the reason for the outcome.

[6]

Donald Trump's Historic Second
Impeachment and Trial

Early in the evening on Election Day 2020, President Trump declared that he had won a "landslide" reelection victory. While every network not long thereafter called the election for Trump's opponent, Joe Biden, Trump told the American people: "This is a fraud on the American public. This is an embarrassment to our country. We were getting ready to win this election. Frankly, we did win this election."[1] Yet by early the next day, November 4, the final votes tallied in the election indicated just the opposite: Trump had lost, including several key swing states that he had won in 2016: Arizona, Georgia, Michigan, Pennsylvania, and Wisconsin.

Trump's frustration at losing reelection increased over the following weeks, and along with that frustration his declarations of election fraud grew increasingly shrill and outlandish. At one point, in a phone call with Georgia's secretary of state and his counsel, Trump urged him to "find 11,780 votes, which is one more than we have."[2] He said they both would be subject to "criminal" action if they did not obey. In the meantime, his friend Rudy Giuliani testified before Michigan's state legislature that he had data showing fraud in the recent election in Michigan, but he never produced any.

Again and again in television appearances, Giuliani repeated claims of voter fraud but never produced evidence.

On December 1, Trump grew furious with United States Attorney General William Barr, who had stood by the president through the Mueller and first impeachment investigations but had confirmed publicly after the election that the Justice Department found no evidence indicating fraud that would have changed the election result. Trump was already angry with Barr for not revealing during the election campaign, as the president had asked, the fact that DOJ was investigating Hunter Biden. Trump's public disparagement convinced Barr to leave the administration. After they met briefly, Trump accepted Barr's resignation.

When the Electoral College certified the election for Biden on December 14, Trump, sitting in the White House fuming, refused to concede. The weekend before, Trump had told Fox News: "I worry about the country having an illegitimate president, that's what I worry about. A president that lost and lost badly."[3] Some Trump electors insisted on meeting after the Electoral College decision, while several Republicans in the House and Senate agreed there had been substantial fraud in the election or that an investigation was needed in Congress to consider challenges to the election outcomes in key states.

On behalf of Trump and his campaign, lawyers filed more than 60 lawsuits challenging the certification of election results in key states that Trump had won in 2016 but lost in 2020. By the end of the year the courts had dismissed them all, and no evidence of the massive fraud Trump or his lawyers claimed ever materialized. In several jurisdictions, Republicans won Senate seats and governorships in the very same election that Trump lost. Trump had no credible explanation for how those Republicans won and he had lost.

Nevertheless, Trump figured he had one last chance on January 6 to turn things around. Congress was scheduled that day to certify the results of the Electoral College, and Trump tried to convince Vice President Mike Pence that Pence had the authority not to accept the results in some states and to order those states to recount and recertify votes. Pence demurred, infuriating Trump by making himself unavailable for any further meetings and conversations that day. As the leaders in both the House and Senate prepared to lead the final certifications in their respective chambers, Trump left the White House to speak at a rally of supporters who had come to Washington, DC, to join his protest against the election's legitimacy. He, Rudy Giuliani, and the conservative lawyer John Eastman (who had tried but failed to connect with the vice president that day) revved up the crowd and urged everyone to march to the Capitol. They did, but they did not stop to protest outside. Instead, they broke through police barriers and smashed locked windows and doors to storm into the Capitol building itself, where they bludgeoned police officers, threatened the lives of Speaker Pelosi and Majority Leader Schumer, among many others, and vandalized or destroyed paintings, statues, desks, and doorways in a frantic search to finish the job that, they believed, the president wanted them to do: stop the steal.

Though Trump wanted to go to the Capitol with the crowd, his Secret Service detail forced him to remain at the

White House. He watched live news feeds of the people riot-ing at the Capitol and made no public statements for more than two hours after the rioting had begun. When he did, he praised the rioters as patriots and declared that he loved them. Some reports indicate that, while Vice President Pence and some of his family had to be rushed to safety at an un-disclosed location, Trump ignored pleas from White House aides and some members of Congress imploring the presi-dent to save Pence's life. Instead, with rioters threatening to "hang Mike Pence," Trump tweeted: "Mike Pence did not have the courage to do what should have been done to pro-tect our country and our Constitution."

After several hours, the rioters were pushed out of the building onto the steps out front. Resolved to complete the electoral vote count by Congress, and to demonstrate deter-mination in the face of insurrection, members of both the House and Senate certified the final results for Joe Biden as the next president. Subsequent reports (and testimony be-fore the House committee formed to investigate the events on January 6) indicated that throughout the afternoon of the riot Trump threw temper tantrums, yelling at aides, try-ing unsuccessfully to be driven to the Capitol, and throwing plates and other items at walls and staff out of frustration over Pence's refusal to help and the failure of his own follow-ers to stop the vote count. In a statement delivered the day after the riot, Trump said he had "immediately ordered the National Guard and federal law enforcement to secure the building and expel the intruders." In fact, the National Guard arrived three hours after the riot had begun, when most of the violence had already subsided. Insiders at the White House reported that, for much of the afternoon on January 6, Trump resisted pleas for help from members of Congress to send reinforcements to the safeguard the Capitol and everyone inside.

I

Impeachment was already on the minds of some members of Congress before the end of the day on January 6. Within days of the insurrection, House Judiciary Committee member Jamie Raskin, Democrat of Maryland, took the lead in drafting a single impeachment article for the House's consideration. Raskin had been a constitutional law professor for more than two decades before his election to the House, and he was strongly motivated to do what he believed his son, who had died tragically just weeks before, would have wanted him to do. He said at the time: "I'm not going to lose my son at the end of 2020 and lose my country and my republic in 2021."[4]

There were several reasons why the House moved in record time to impeach Trump without holding hearings or conducting an investigation. First, Trump's term was set to end in less than three weeks. Rushing to judgment was hardly cost-free, but Trump's leaving office was bound to make it harder, if not impossible, to reach him through the impeachment process. At the very least, the impeachment would begin before he left office, enabling members of Congress to defend extending the impeachment as a logical consequence of the fact that the Constitution did not expressly dictate the timing or bar the House and Senate from performing their constitutional duties. Second, many House members had no need to investigate, because they were among the people the rioters had threatened. They also had plenty of media videos, not to mention the Congress's own video records, showing rioters ripping through the Capitol and trying to chase down congressional leaders for punishment. Third, the House was compelled to do something, or risk looking weak (if not completely powerless), to protect itself from people bent on destroying the Capitol or hanging the Speaker or other officials. And finally, the Speaker and other Democratic leaders did not want to give Republican members a platform to attack the election outcome and the investigation. Ironically, Republican House members had been under attack themselves, and the Democratic leadership might have figured that the more quickly they moved, the better chance they had of picking up some Republican support before the anger and emotions from January 6 dissipated. In short, the House struck while the iron was still hot.

The impeachment article charged Trump with "inciting violence against the government of the United States." Though the January 6 committee convened by the House would later uncover more evidence of what happened and what the president did that day, Representative Raskin included references to various incidents throughout the day that supported the charge of insurrection against Donald Trump, including citing his false claims of election fraud, his phone call with Georgia's secretary of state, and urging his crowd of supporters to take action or risk losing their country through incendiary statements (including "If you don't fight like hell you're not going to have a country anymore").

This article of impeachment broke new ground in two ways. First, it was the first time in history the House considered and approved only one impeachment article against a president. There were ten impeachment articles approved by the House against Johnson and two against Bill Clinton, but never before had the House put its entire case into a single article directed against a president. Second, the article referenced, for the first time ever in any impeachment, section 3 of the Fourteenth Amendment: "Further," it read, "section 3 of the Fourteenth Amendment to the United States Constitution prohibits any person who has 'engaged in insurrection or rebellion against' the United States from 'hold[ing] any office . . . under the United States.'"[5] Never before had section 3 of the Fourteenth Amendment, which was passed in the aftermath of the Civil War to prevent the potential return to power of former Confederates, been invoked against a president, and the remainder of the proceedings wrestled with the question of what it meant and whether it applied to Trump.

The House did not vote strictly on party lines. On January 13, 10 Republicans, along with all House Democrats, voted to approve the article, the largest number of representatives ever to vote to impeach a president from the same party. The ten included Liz Cheney, a conservative representative from Wyoming and daughter of former Vice President Dick Cheney. All ten faced death threats and calls for reprisals from other Republicans in the House. (In mid-May, Cheney was stripped of her position in the House leadership.)

Criticism of and support for the impeachment article came from both sides of the aisle. Many Democrats saw the impeachment effort as a waste of time because of Trump's likely acquittal in the Senate and as a distraction from Biden's first weeks in office. Many claimed that impeaching Trump had the disadvantage of making the first piece of business for incoming Vice President Kamala Harris awkward, as she undoubtedly would try to avoid being seen presiding over the trial of her election rival. Republicans denounced the impeachment as nothing more than a last-ditch effort to embarrass Trump and to "relitigate" the past. Meanwhile, several prominent conservatives, who had been silent throughout the first Trump impeachment, expressed support for impeaching him for his role in the January 6 storming of the Capitol. Polling showed that 56% of Americans favored impeaching Trump a second time.

II

This time, the Speaker was not responsible for the delay in initiating the Senate trial. Technically, the Senate was not in session, and Majority Leader Mitch McConnell said that unanimous consent was needed to end the recess, but none would be forthcoming. In addition, both McConnell and Chuck Schumer, Democrat of New York, who would become the new Majority Leader on the day of Joe Biden's inauguration, acknowledged that the trial could not start immediately. Each said at least two weeks were needed for the Senate to prepare for the trial. Moreover, Schumer as well as President-elect Biden were concerned that the trial would divert attention from Biden's inauguration, the inauguration of the first woman of color as vice president, and their first hundred days in office. Further, the delay ensured that, when the trial did begin, Trump would no longer be in office, triggering a significant question of whether the Constitution allowed post-presidential impeachment. It was one of several procedural and substantive questions that awaited the Senate once it received the article of impeachment.

Even before the trial started, the Senate confronted an unusual question. Everyone understood from the first Trump impeachment trial that the Chief Justice of the United States should preside, as required by the Constitution. But many wondered whether Chief Justice Roberts would preside over Trump's second trial. If he did not, the next person in line to preside was Vice President Harris, who understandably would be reluctant, in her first days in office, to preside over the trial of the presidential candidate who lost.

Largely through back channels, the Chief Justice made clear he had no interest in presiding and rebuffed all entreaties to do so. The vice president also made clear her choice when she immediately passed on the opportunity. This left the position of presiding officer to the Senate Pro Tempore, the senior member of the majority party in the Senate, who was Senator Patrick Leahy of Vermont. After agreeing to serve, Leahy took several steps to show the Senate that he intended to put aside his party affiliation and to be evenhanded and fair to both sides. Both he and Majority Leader Schumer agreed to restrict communications between Leahy and Democratic members of the Senate. It was understood that Leahy and his staff would communicate only with the Majority Leader, and even then only for official business that would also require the participation of the Minority Leader (now Mitch McConnell). Leahy vowed: "When I preside over the impeachment trial of former President Donald Trump, I will not waver from constitutional and sworn obligations to administer the trial with fairness, in accordance with the Constitution and the Laws."[6]

Leahy thus became the fourth person and the first Senate Pro Tempore to preside over a presidential impeachment trial. In the trial that followed, perhaps his most controversial decision was made early on. He declared that he would follow the precedent set by other Senate Pro Tempores who presided over non-impeachment trials, ruled on procedural and evidentiary matters, and also cast individual votes on such matters as a member of the Senate. Leahy told the *New York Times*: "I've presided hundreds of times [on other legislative business]—I don't know how many rulings I've made. I've never had anyone, Republican or Democrat, say my rulings were unfair. That is what the presiding officer is supposed to do."[7]

Trump, no longer in office, could not rely on government lawyers to defend him. He hired two prominent litigators from South Carolina to represent him, but he soon fired them when they did not agree to ground his defense on claims of election fraud. He then hired three lawyers—Bruce Castor, a former district attorney of Montgomery County,

Pennsylvania; David Schoen, a civil rights lawyer from Alabama; and Michael van der Veen, a criminal defense lawyer from Philadelphia. More than a few Republican senators shared during the trial and afterward that the three Trump lawyers were ineffective. In his first presentation at the trial, Castor launched into rambling, nearly incoherent musings that included puzzling comments about Ben Sasse, a Republican senator from Nebraska who prior to the trial had been subject to censure back home from his own party for having criticized the "weird worship of one dude."

The new set of House Managers was more harmonious than the first set in 2020. Besides Jamie Raskin, Speaker Pelosi appointed eight other Democrats as House Managers, several of whom were former prosecutors: Eric Swalwell of California, Ted Lieu of California, and Stacey Plaskett (a former Justice Department official who was not allowed to vote in the House proceedings because she was a delegate who represented the Virgin Islands). The team also included Hakeem Jeffries, who in 2022 would succeed Pelosi as the leader of the Democrats in the House. Even Republican senators who voted against conviction later acknowledged that the House Managers had done an excellent job presenting the case.

Once the trial commenced on January 26 and Senator Leahy was sworn in as the presiding officer, the Senate confronted several important procedural and substantive questions of constitutional law. The first arose on the first day when Senator Rand Paul, a Republican from Kentucky, raised a point of order contesting the constitutionality of the procedures for the trial, including Leahy as presiding officer. The ensuing debate was brief, partly because senators—and many outside pundits and experts—had been pondering for weeks the question of who should preside. Paul's point was that the Chief Justice should preside because the charge was based on Trump's actions as president and accordingly he should be entitled to the same safeguards that apply whenever a president is placed on trial in the Senate. A second concern may have been Paul's doubting whether anyone but the Chief Justice could be trusted to be evenhanded in presiding over the trial. This insistence that the Chief Justice must preside could have been a way for the Senate GOP to show that the rightful president of the United States was still Donald Trump.

The rebuttal was short and simple: The Chief Justice presided over presidential impeachment trials, and Trump was no longer president. In this country, only one person at a time gets to be president, and the president at the time of Trump's second trial was Joe Biden.

After a brief debate, the Senate voted 56 to 44 to table Paul's point of order, with five Republican senators joining all 50 Democratic senators. A briefing schedule was established. On February 8, Majority Leader Schumer and Minority Leader McConnell agreed on procedures, which included giving the sides up to 16 hours each to make their case, debate, and call witnesses. The Senate voted 89 to 11 to accept the rules for the trial, which was set to begin the next day.

The first day of trial began with a second important vote. Senators were asked to consider the constitutionality of the trial itself, specifically whether the Senate had the power or jurisdiction to hold an impeachment trial for someone who was no longer president and who had returned to private life. A four-hour debate ensued.

The House Managers cited several precedents in which the Senate held impeachment trials for officials who were impeached but no longer in office. Among them was the very first impeachment trial, in which the first Senate voted to retain jurisdiction over the trial of William Blount, who had been expelled from the Senate before his impeachment by the House. The Senate proceeded with the trial nonetheless but eventually acquitted Blount largely on the ground that members of Congress were not impeachable officials. A second precedent involved the impeachment of West Humphreys, who had resigned as a federal judge in 1861 to join the Confederacy. A year later the House impeached him, and the Senate convicted and removed him from the office he had already abandoned. Yet another precedent involved William Belknap, the secretary of war under President Ulysses S. Grant. After the House impeached Belknap for bribery, he rushed over to the White House, where he resigned from his cabinet post in an attempt to forestall any trial in the Senate. The Senate, voting 37 to 29, held that Belknap was "amenable to trial by impeachment [notwithstanding] his resignation of said office."

The House Managers argued that a major reason for these precedents and for allowing the Senate's impeachment trial to proceed was that, if no trial were possible, presidents could not be held accountable through impeachment for misconduct during their last few days, months, or weeks in office; in short they could abuse power without consequence. Barring post-presidential impeachment trials, therefore, meant that presidents could remain in office through impeachment proceedings in the House and, then, if it appeared as if conviction were likely in the Senate, they could resign to stop the trial and preserve their eligibility to run or serve again as president or in some other federal office.

Trump's lawyers and Minority Leader McConnell argued that the process applied only to people who held certain offices and that, upon leaving office, they became private citizens who were no longer subject to the impeachment process. They derided the argument that impeachment trials had to be allowed to proceed or risk extensive presidential abuses of power as the "Raskin rule" because Rep. Raskin spoke of the dangers of allowing presidents a free pass to engage in misconduct in their last few weeks or months in office. They relied on the plain text of the Constitution specifically naming "Presidents, Vice-Presidents and all civil officers of the United States" as the set of impeachable officials, raising the inference, in their judgment, that only people currently serving in those office were subject to impeachment. Professor Cass Sunstein of Harvard Law School and Michael Luttig, a well-respected conservative who had served as a federal appellate judge, were among the many authorities who agreed with the arguments made by Trump's lawyers. When the matter came to a vote, the Senate voted 56 to 44 that it had proper jurisdiction over Trump's impeachment. Six Republicans joined all Democrats in recognizing the legitimacy of the trial. Senators were left free to decide for themselves later whether to feel bound by—to follow or disregard—the Senate's decision regarding jurisdiction.

Another major question up for debate was whether Trump had committed an impeachable offense. His lawyers argued that the impeachment was based on his speech at the January 6 rally, which was protected by the First Amendment. He cannot be punished for protected speech, they argued. Moreover, the lawyers contended that impeachable offenses had to be crimes, and that the elements of the crime of incitement had not been proved.

Led by Raskin, the House Managers made two responses. First, they reminded the Senate that impeachable offenses did not have to be actual crimes or include criminal acts. The article focused on abuse of power, and abuses of power were legitimate grounds for impeachment. Second, Raskin made the point that the First Amendment did not protect Trump because his speech and conduct violated his oath of office. Raskin cited a memorandum from the Federalist Society (the organization providing Trump recommendations for Supreme Court candidates) stating that "[t]he First Amendment is no bar to the Senate convicting former president Trump and disqualifying him from holding future office."[8]

The Senate also debated the basic fairness of the trial. One of the constant refrains from Trump's lawyers was that the trial did not satisfy due process. On February 12, 2021, Trump lawyer David Schoen argued before the Senate that "[o]ur Constitution and any basic sense of fairness require that every legal process with significant consequences for a person's life, including impeachment, requires due process under the law, which includes fact-finding, and the establishment of a legitimate evidentiary record with an appropriate foundation." Another Trump lawyer, Michael van der Veen, similarly argued to the Senate that "[t]he due process clause applies to [an] impeachment hearing, and it's been severely and extremely violated."[9]

The argument was largely made for its political appeal to Trump's base and to Trump himself. There were many problems with the argument that due process applied or was violated, beginning with the facts that impeachments were not "legal proceedings" but rather unique political proceedings; that no protected life, liberty, or property due process interests were at stake or being violated; and finally that Trump had received lots of process, including being able to call his own witnesses, cross-examine the government's witnesses, and put into evidence nearly anything he wished.

The final vote was on Saturday, February 13. To no one's surprise, the Senate failed to convict Trump, with the final tally falling short of the two-thirds threshold for conviction. Yet to nearly everyone's surprise, seven Republicans joined all Democrats in voting 57 to 43 to convict Trump. It was the largest number of senators to vote to convict a president in an impeachment trial and the largest number of senators to vote to convict a president from their own party.

Almost immediately after the trial adjourned, Minority Leader Mitch McConnell took to the Senate floor to unleash a blistering attack on Trump. "There's no question—none," McConnell said, "that President Trump is practically and morally responsible for provoking the events of that day." He explained that he had voted against conviction because "[w]e have no power to convict and disqualify a former office holder who is now a private citizen." (Trump responded by calling Mc-Connell a "political hack," while Republican senators ignored Trump's request to drop McConnell as their leader in the Senate.) Indeed, more than 67 senators issued public statements after the trial, nearly all excoriating the former president for his misconduct.

Throughout the 2016 presidential campaign and the following four years, Trump dodged recordings and newspaper stories that reported his abusing women, lying to the American people, and consorting with racists and criminals, denying everything as "fake news." But at the end of his second trial, the patience, support, and ardor of many of Trump's former supporters dissolved. The statements of trusted Republican senators, the videos of the violence at the Capitol (including rioters looking to hang the vice president and to hurt, if not kill, the Speaker of the House), Trump's own entreaties to the crowd to go to the Capitol, and his megalomaniacal declarations of the election having been stolen from him eroded what was once rock-solid support from many Republicans.

III

The constitutional ramifications of Trump's second impeachment are still being felt and debated. His second impeachment established the strongest precedent yet for post-presidential impeachment. It was the sixth time that the Senate had voted in favor of its jurisdiction over the trial of someone who had left office in the interim. In the trials of Blount, Belknap, and now Trump, the Senate voted that it had jurisdiction over the respective impeachments; the Senate continued with the trials of West Humphreys (1862), George English (1929), and Robert Archbald (1912) for misconduct in offices they no longer occupied.

An additional argument supporting post-presidential impeachment did not get much airtime during the trial but bears emphasis. The argument that presidents are amenable to impeachment only while in office ignores one of the fundamental purposes of impeachment: to serve as the only means to address misconduct for which the law provided no remedy. Thus, suggesting that presidents could not still be held liable after leaving office for impeachable offenses missed the point entirely of the Constitution's establishing impeachment to address presidential abuses of power committed during their term of office. In other words, it is not true that after a president leaves office he may still be liable at law for his misconduct. A president's abuse of power is by definition a violation of the Constitution that is not redressable in a legal proceeding, whether civil or criminal. The only venue for addressing presidential abuse of power is the impeachment process. In addition, whatever *legal* sanctions Trump faced after leaving office for his involvement with the storming of the Capitol involve different claims, burdens of proof, and sanctions than the Constitution addresses through the impeachment process.

Yet Trump's second trial was the fourth time that the Senate had acquitted a president of impeachable misconduct. It reinforced the perception of impeachment's ineffectiveness as a check on presidential misconduct. Once again, senators from the president's party were sufficiently united to preclude any possibility of reaching the threshold for conviction. This outcome was especially discouraging because there could be no doubt that the president's incitement of an insurrection against the Capitol would, if proven, be an impeachable offense. Yet Trump emerged unrepentant and even more determined to settle scores with people he considered to be political enemies. On November 15, 2022, Trump announced his intention to run for the presidency a third time.

Trump did not emerge from the trial entirely unscathed, however. Two impeachments damaged his legacy, if not his standing in the GOP, and dozens of senators, many from his own party, denounced his misconduct, staining his presidency and reputation. Throughout the second impeachment, the fact that a slim majority of Americans agreed that their senators should vote to convict Trump reinforced both the legitimacy and sting of the impeachment. (The revelations of the January 6 committee in 2022 undoubtedly damaged his standing further.) Trump's second trial was the first time most Americans favored convicting a president through an impeachment trial.

As a result, the imperial presidency did not emerge untainted either from Trump's second encounter with impeachment. By the time the second trial began, Trump no longer controlled the levers of the presidency; and Joe Biden waived executive privilege over many of the documents (such as the White House visitor log) that Trump had previously refused to share with Congress. While most Republicans supported Trump's robust exercise of power as president, even to undermine congressional inquiries, they would not grant the same respect to Biden as president. Thus, their support for the imperial presidency while Trump was in office appeared opportunistic rather than genuine. If Republican senators abandoned the unitary theory of the executive when it no longer served their political interests, it cannot have been much of a constitutional principle to begin with.

The second impeachment also launched a nationwide debate over the meaning of section 3 of the Fourteenth Amendment. Prior to the second trial, little attention, in academia and the media, had been paid to the provision. Adopted in 1868, section 3 provides: "No person shall be a Senator or Representative in Congress, or elector of President or Vice-President, or hold any office, civil or military, under the United States . . . who, having previously taken oath, as a member of Congress, or as an officer of the United States, . . . to support the Constitution of the United States, shall have engaged in insurrection or rebellion against the same, or given aid or comfort to the enemies thereof." Given the interest many Democratic members had in applying this section to Trump, several legal questions have arisen, including what kinds of activities trigger the section, what offices the section applies to, and the kinds of mechanisms required to determine or enforce disqualification or ineligibility. I provide such questions below.

First, it seems obvious that section 3 was designed for the era of Reconstruction when Confederates were attempting to return to power or seek federal office. For the most part, section 3 was used only for the short period between its ratification in 1868 and the enactment of the Amnesty Act of 1872. The latter removed a disqualification that had previously been imposed on Confederates and was enacted by the two-thirds supermajority required in section 3. And the fact remains that section 3 has not been invoked since 1919, when the Senate tried but failed to prevent the seating of a congressman whose conviction for espionage was thrown out by the Supreme Court.

A second issue with section 3: To whom does it apply? Presidents are not expressly included among the specific officers mentioned in section 3. That omission is consistent with some scholarship suggesting that presidents occupy a unique office created by the Constitution and are not "officers of the United States."[10] There is no helpful legislative history indicating whether presidents' treacherous conduct is confined to the impeachment process; however, if so, that would seem to make even stronger the need for impeachment to have been used in Trump's case. Otherwise he would have avoided having to account for his misconduct before any other authority.

Third, section 3 does not make clear how it should be implemented. It hardly seems self-executing, because some determination must be made about insurrection or rebellion (though the section is silent about who has that authority). Criminal prosecutions might be appropriate for making such determinations, although the burden of proof (beyond a reasonable doubt) is of course the toughest that the law employs.

Fourth, during the debate over the reach of section 3, many Republican senators and commentators rediscovered original meaning. Despite having insisted that the GOP's Supreme Court nominees prioritized original meaning above all other sources of constitutional meaning, Republicans in the House and Senate had not cited, much less relied on, original meaning in opposing the second impeachment of Trump. But in the second trial they argued that section 3 was intended to apply to only Confederates who were attempting to be elected to or occupy federal offices after the Civil War. The failure to convict Trump was understood by some as a rejection of the Democratic majority's reading of section 3.

Nevertheless, the failure of Republican senators, Trump's lawyers, and Trump himself to ground their arguments or defense in original meaning during his second impeachment trial reveals the hypocrisy of their earlier statements about its foundation as the only legitimate source, besides the text itself, of constitutional decision-making. When original meaning did not support their desired result, they ignored it. When it could be used to narrow the scope of the meaning of section 3 of the Fourteenth Amendment, it became useful again.

The point is not that Republicans monopolized hypocrisy in debating the Constitution. The point is that it is easy to filter out weak theories of constitutional interpretation if they are used only when they benefit one party or president and then dropped or ignored for presidents from the opposing party. The real test of constitutional commitment is whether it is followed, regardless of the side it benefits or hurts. If a principle depends on the name and party of the occupant of the White House, then it is not a principle. It is political preference disguised as principle.

Fifth, Trump's second impeachment brought attention to the Twenty-Fifth Amendment, which provides a process for suspending presidents. As the House was deliberating whether to impeach Trump a second time, Speaker Pelosi sent a letter to Vice President Pence "to convene and mobilize the Cabinet to activate the 25th Amendment to declare the President incapable of executing the duties of his office."[11] The next day, Pence responded that the mechanism for temporarily suspending a president for disability, as set forth in the Twenty-Fifth Amendment, should not be used "as a means of punishment or usurpation." Pelosi had said that, if Pence were to initiate the procedures set forth in the Twenty-Fifth Amendment for suspending a president because of mental or physical disability, the House's impeachment of Trump would not go forward. Given Pence's position, the House impeached Trump two days later.

Pence was almost certainly correct in his construction of the Twenty-Fifth Amendment. It is not impeachment-lite. Rather, the Twenty-Fifth Amendment was designed to address a situation in which a president lacks the capacity to carry out the duties of his office. It was not meant for the circumstances confronting Congress and the nation in the aftermath of the storming of the Capitol, a situation in which the president was being accused of deliberately violating his oath of office, thereby encouraging insurrection and posing a danger to the republic (as charged in the impeachment article). Indeed, history will reflect that the article alleged Trump "willfully made statements that, in context, encouraged—and foreseeably resulted in—lawless action at the Capitol." In other words, Democrats charged that Trump would not do his job properly, something perfectly suited for consideration in the impeachment process.

Finally, it is in the nature of the commentariat to second-guess, and there was plenty of second-guessing both impeachments of Trump. But not all of it was sour grapes. In an insightful op-ed, Michael McConnell, a respected conservative scholar and former judge, argued that the Democrats would have been better served had they drafted the impeachment article differently. He argued that the "House should have crafted a broader and less legalistic set of charges" rather than focusing on incitement, which led to the House "unnecessarily shoulder[ing] the burden of proving elements of that crime." The terms "invited the defense to respond in the same legalistic terms presented by the House impeachment managers."

Michael McConnell's analysis makes eminent sense. While he concedes (as do I) that perhaps refining the article would have made no practical difference, making the charges broader would have made the defense's job harder. Drafting the article in simpler, broader terms is perfectly appropriate because impeachable offenses do not have to be indictable crimes. Trump did many things wrong that day and in the days before: destroying documents; refusing to do his duty to order protection for members of Congress and the vice president; spreading falsehoods about the election; trying to intimidate the vice president and members of Congress and Georgia's secretary of state to do what he demanded; and using his personal phone or others' phones to engage in communications that could not be traced directly back to him. As Michael McConnell wrote: "The charges should have encompassed Mr. Trump's use of the mob and other tactics to intimidate government officials to void the election results[] and his dereliction of duty by failing to try to end the violence in the hours after" returning to the White following his speech at the rally.[12]

A simple description of what Trump did wrong during his last months in office should have justified his second impeachment. Yet the House did not do that. It persisted to craft impeachment articles as if they were indictments. Presumably, many House members insisted on emphasizing the element of criminality, even though it is not constitutionally necessary. Impeachment is fundamentally about a president's abuse of power or breach of the trust that the Constitution has placed in the president as manifest in the oath each president takes upon becoming president.

Epilogue

The Future of Presidential Impeachment

Presidential impeachments are stress tests for the Congress, presidency, American people, and Constitution. While the country has endured through each of these ordeals, many people have felt the federal impeachment process has proven ineffective because of several developments.

The first is the practically impossible constitutional threshold for conviction. All four presidential impeachment trials have ended with the president being acquitted. Only one (Andrew Johnson) came anywhere close to being convicted and removed from office. Otherwise, one popular president and a divisive president (twice) with a loyal base of support fell well short of conviction, removal, and disqualification.

The second is a rise of extreme partisanship dictating that the goal of each party is to destroy the other. The framers did not expect political parties to flourish, much less to have generated more fidelity to them than to the Constitution itself or the institutions it established. The development is incompatible with the system that James Madison and the other framers had envisioned: a system premised, as the Constitution had been, on negotiation, compromise, and the effectiveness of a variety of checking mechanisms to ensure that no single branch or faction ever became beyond the reach of the law or the Constitution.

The rise of extreme partisanship has hardly been lost on presidents. It has benefited them because it provided leverage to block impeachment. When the next presidential impeachment happens, the president will know that, so long as he keeps the members of his party in Congress largely united in opposing impeachment, he can avoid any sanction at the trial. This will be true for any president, regardless of party and popularity, and thus the thing to watch for in the future is how united the president can keep his party in opposing impeachment and conviction.

Third, the office of the presidency has changed, especially in the twentieth century. From the beginning of the republic through the nineteenth century, presidents did much of their work on their own, including interviewing and meeting with job applicants. They had no press secretary or teams of lawyers on call. When Richard Nixon was president, the White House Counsel's office had only one person, John Dean, though he had teams of assistants who acted as shields against the scrutiny of the press and Congress. Nixon was widely associated with the imperial presidency, which increasingly has become an institution teeming with lawyers, assistants, and other staff who speak for the presidency, publicize and package his narrative of events, and run interference against challenges to his authority. The presidency is no longer a single person but an institution, one that is hard to topple. Andrew Johnson may have had a small team of lawyers defending him during his impeachment trial, but Richard Nixon, Bill Clinton, and Donald Trump led an institution that was devoted to keeping them in office.

To be successful in the postmodern era and in the future, impeachments must break through a phalanx of institutions that serve the presidency, including the president's party, press officials, lawyers from inside and outside the office of the presidency, and the administration writ large, including cabinet officers such as the Attorney General, and the heads of the FBI and CIA, serving at the pleasure of the president. As Trump's first impeachment demonstrated, his hold over his administration was sufficiently strong to block congressional subpoenas and meaningful public and press scrutiny. The effect of his acquittal was to reinforce his determination to staff the administration with loyalists; many of them stood by his side during the storming of the Capitol and proved impotent to get help to the members of Congress, including leaders of his own party, he had abandoned that day for hours. When the election was finally certified the next day, it had been done without the help of his administration. Indeed, for months before that, his administration blocked the release of funding for the transition to Joe Biden's administration. When the institution of the presidency is corrupt or devoted to the maintenance of corruption more than it is to the rule of law, impeachment is not the only casualty.

Fourth, the rise of the internet and 24-7 social media has upended the information ecosystem that democracy needs to survive. James Madison was one of many framers who believed that the intricate system of checks and balances built into the Constitution depended on the public's growing interest in being educated about government and policymaking. "I go on this great republican principle, that the people will have virtue and intelligence to select men of virtue and wisdom," he wrote. The proliferation of online media outlets enables people to consult news sources that hew to, or reflect, their opinions, but it has not forced them to confront, or learn from, opinions different than theirs or facilitated the search for any objective truth. This tendency reinforces the extreme partisanship that pushes people back into their comfortable niches—and the so-called facts that are shaped by news sources rather than actual events.

The fifth development undermining the effectiveness of impeachment is the Seventeenth Amendment, which changed the original scheme for selecting senators. When the framers created the Senate, they initially sought to insulate it from the vicissitudes of public opinion. To that end they included a provision whereby senators would be selected by their respective state legislatures, which could then instruct them on how to vote and recall them if they failed to do as directed. This approach rarely produced a Senate disposed to the long view, one that sought to rise above petty partisanship. Ratified in 1913, the Seventeenth Amendment replaced the original scheme with one that guarantees direct political pressure or support from the senators' constituents.

And finally, presidential impeachments are rooted in culture. Culture plays an instrumental role in shaping the values of greatest concern to the Congress and the American people. A culture that does not uniformly frown at marital infidelities or regards presidential lies as unimportant is hardly going to ram through the conviction of a president who has been guilty of such things. A culture sharply riven by partisan and tribal differences is not likely to reach the threshold for convicting a president who champions one side or the other in the culture wars.

The coarsening of public debate has been a result of cultural developments assisted by social media, which feeds off and amplifies the differences dividing the nation. The rise of infotainment and soft news—speculation and commentary—has fostered an environment in which shouting and personal attacks substitute for the civil dialogue that the framers had hoped would sustain the republic. Increasingly, the antics on cable news programs, aimed at entertaining and energizing the party base, are not confined to the airwaves. Donald Trump was often said to have led a "performative presidency": he obsessed over how he rated on television and cared deeply about generating images and sound bites for his base through the media, especially Fox News. More than a few Republican members of Congress took their lead from Trump and modeled their own behavior on his. The results that mattered were ratings and airtime, regardless of the ramifications for the institutions of the presidency and the Senate.

If the impeachment process is broken, it is because of these developments. The impulse of many scholars and commentators to push for increasing the power of the Chief Justice when presiding over a presidential impeachment trial is but one example of how some people have sought in vain to reduce or displace congressional discretion over presidential impeachment. Distrust of Congress has been counterbalanced, at least by some, with greater confidence in the Chief Justice as a neutral decision maker. The difficulty is that the framers already made the choice to vest Congress, not the Chief Justice, with the "sole" power over the impeachment process and thus the key substantive and procedural decisions within that process.

While there is no easy answer as to how (or even whether) it is possible to fix the impeachment process, a few possibilities are clear: First, if we shift our perspectives, impeachment may not necessarily be as ineffective as it appears. Although four presidential impeachment trials resulted in acquittals, we overlook the extent to which the prospect of impeachment has possibly curbed some presidential misconduct. For example, President Trump reluctantly declined to fire Special Counsel Robert Mueller for fear it might have triggered an impeachment. Trump and Nixon might have followed the same logic when deciding not to pardon themselves. Other decisions might have been made over the centuries to forego certain misconduct to avoid impeachment or the condemnation of history.

Second, nothing important within the impeachment process can change unless the underlying culture changes. Culture imbues and shapes the values that guide not only public decision-making but also decision-making within Congress, especially on matters of significant social concern. Such matters as valuing truth, civility, transparency, and curbing public corruption (and self-dealing, bribery, and extortion) count only insofar as they are embedded within our culture. If the culture rewards or promotes misconduct, then misconduct prevails; any checking mechanisms within the Constitution are doomed because of the failure of will and virtue.

Third, education holds the greatest promise for the Constitution's durability. The founders believed that education could inculcate values for America's survival. Like Madison, Abraham Lincoln believed that education was the government's most important responsibility and that educated voters would understand the stakes of elections and rise above self-interest and rank partisanship. Without education, or leaders, or a public that values democracy, democracy dies.

The media plays an indispensable role in educating the public and keeping leaders in check. The media holds the greatest promise for asking the questions that need to be asked and for placing a spotlight on dangers to democracy. If political parties do not care about truth or the viability of democracy, then it is the media's job to make the people care; it can do so by pressing leaders (inside and outside government) for simple answers to easy questions that arise with every presidential impeachment. What evidence do they believe and why? They do not have to be pressed on questions about what qualifies as impeachable misconduct. Instead the questions can address the misconduct itself. For example: Was Trump's behavior toward the leader of Ukraine "perfect"? If so, why? If not, why not? Did Trump handle the storming of the Capitol perfectly? If so, why? If not, what problems were there in his performance then or later? Lawyers, like the media, belong to an evidence-based profession. When a former president claims election fraud, what actual evidence is there for the claim? With Republicans retaking control of the House in January 2023 following the November 2022 election (albeit by a slim margin), many of them threatened to impeach Joe Biden. Some promised another investigation into his only surviving son, Hunter. They should be asked about any evidence regarding the abuse of power by President Biden. What did he know and when did he know it? Why were the bipartisan investigations undertaken by the Senate Foreign Relations Committee on these matters insufficient? The answers that matter are the ones with evidence. Otherwise, it is bluster.

If the answers to these questions are not about the impeached president or the president facing impeachment, but instead about the supposed misconduct of other presidents from a different party, we do not have to be political rocket scientists to recognize that those answers are partisan hype. If a president got away with wrongdoing, then his fate has nothing to do with the law of presidential impeachment. Either a president facing impeachment has done something wrong or he has not. The same could be said for recklessly speeding during my commute into work. If I am caught speeding in a school zone and my defense is that the same cop allowed another driver to speed a few days ago, that is no defense at all. I either drove above the speed limit or did not. The president either did something wrong or did not. And if we cannot get a straight answer to that question, then whatever is blocking our inquiry is a problem that has little or nothing to do with the president's misconduct.

Much of this is to say that, however ineffective the practice of presidential impeachment has been, the law of presidential impeachment is clear and always has been. It addresses presidential abuse of power for which there is no legal remedy. And if the mechanism of impeachment cannot be made to focus on such misconduct, then "the fault," to quote Shakespeare, is not "in our stars" or even the Constitution "but in ourselves." The Constitution makes impeachment difficult, but it does not make it impossible. America's leaders are only as good, or as uncorrupt, as the American people allow them to be.

ACKNOWLEDGMENTS

Early in the evening of January 5, 2021, I left Washington after meeting with officials about presidential misconduct in obstructing the peaceful transfer of power. Within days, Senator Patrick Leahy brought me back to be a part of his team when he presided over the second impeachment trial of Donald J. Trump.

In the meantime, the Capitol had become nearly unrecognizable. The entire Capitol, including Senate offices, were surrounded by tall steel fences; hundreds of National Guard troops were monitoring checkpoints and the perimeter. After having been allowed entry into the area outside the Senate buildings, I was escorted into the Senate's office buildings, where I received an ID pass and made my way to the offices of Senator Leahy. For the next few weeks I came and went, always under the friendly but watchful eyes of the National Guard and Capitol Police.

Every day during the trial that followed I saw evidence of the wreckage wrought by Donald Trump's destructive incitement. Later one former White House aide described how Trump threw his lunch against a White House wall in frustration over Attorney General William Barr's debunking Trump's fantasy that he had won the 2020 presidential election. But on January 6, Trump threw his supporters against the Capitol and members of Congress to thwart the election's final certification. Far from being innocent tourists (as several Republican members of Congress maintained), they tried to wreck the Capitol.

I saw the broken windows and doors. I saw the defaced artwork and statues. Each day I saw the Capitol Police, who graciously guarded us as we conducted the business of the Constitution. To those officers—and dutiful National Guardsmen—I salute your patriotism, fidelity to duty, and bravery. I was proud to be an American before I joined Senator Leahy's team. I was an even prouder American when I returned home to my family.

I am profoundly thankful for my family's encouragement and support during the second trial of Donald Trump and the writing of *The Law of Presidential Impeachment*. They make everything I do meaningful. I could not have completed this book, or completed the public service I was assigned, without their love and support.

Impeachment has bookended my life. I watched the Watergate hearings in high school. I testified twice during House Judiciary Committee hearings on presidential impeachment. I have had the honor to research and write two books and more than a dozen articles about the law of impeachment. There are honors for which I am grateful. Speaking to the House of Representatives about the history of impeachment. Serving as a legal analyst for CNN while covering two presidential impeachments. And the capstone to my career to date: serving as Senator Leahy's special counsel in the second trial of Donald Trump.

I am truly honored and grateful, to have worked with so many dedicated House members and lawyers on the law of presidential impeachment. This includes but is not limited to current and past representatives: Charles Canady, John Conyers, William Delahunt, Jim Leach, Sheila Jackson Lee, Zoe Lofgren, Jamie Raskin, Mary Gay Scanlon, Bobby Scott, and David Skaggs. The Senate staffs I joined and worked with could not have been more generous in welcoming me to contribute meaningfully to their important work. These experiences have informed my understanding of the law and practice of presidential impeachment.

The University of North Carolina School of Law supported my research on the law of presidential impeachment. The UNC Law Library, especially its superb research staff, were indispensable to the completion of this book. Indispensable as well was the excellent research assistance I received from a number of UNC law students (now graduates), including Rachel Grossman, Rachel Jennings, and Hailey Klabo.

When I first began studying and writing about the impeachment process, in the 1980s, I had no idea what the future held, either for impeachment or for my career. Since then I have had many opportunities to do more than just research the subject; I have experienced the impeachment process from the inside. All this has made me a better teacher, scholar, and lawyer. And while I do not know when there will be another presidential impeachment, I am sure that there will be one in our future, assuming the constitutional order holds. When that day comes, I hope that this book will become a useful resource for the people charged with understanding and implementing the Constitution's most important process for holding presidents accountable for their misconduct.

NOTES

PREFACE

1 Statement of Hon. Barbara Jordan, a Representative in Congress from the 18th Congressional District of the State of Texas ("My faith in the constitution is whole . . ."), Debate on Articles of Impeachment Hearings of the Committee on the Judiciary, House of Representatives, Ninety-Third Congress, Second Session, July 24, 1974.

2 Alexander Hamilton, The Federalist Papers, No. 65.

3 Joseph Story, Commentaries on the Constitution, section 788, 256 (1833).

4 Raoul Berger, Impeachment: The Constitutional Problems 88 (1974) (citation omitted).

5 Michael J. Gerhardt, The Federal Impeachment Process: A Constitutional and Historical Analysis 21 (rev. ed. 2019) (citation omitted).

6 Charles Black, Impeachment: A Handbook (1974).

7 591 US __ (2020).

1. HOW IMPEACHMENT WORKS

* Source: https://constitution.congress.gov/constitution/article-2.

1 A. Hamilton, T he Federalist Papers, No. 70.

2 Declaration of Independence, July 4, 1776.

3 U.S. Const., art. II, section 4.

4 Id.

5 William Blackstone, Commentaries on the Laws of England, Chapter Six: Of High Treason (1765–69).

6 U.S. Const., art. I, section 3, clause 7.

7 U.S. Const., art. I, section 2.

8 U.S. Const., art. I, section 3.

9 Id.

10 Id.

11 U.S. Const., art. I, section 3, clause 6.

12 U.S. Const., art. I, section 5, clause 2.

13 U.S. Const., art. III, section 3, clause 1.

14 Akhil Amar, Intratextualism, 112 Harv. L. Rev. 747 (1999).

15 Impeachable Offenses: Historical Background, U.S. Constitution Annotated, Article II, Section 4.

16 James Wilson, Lectures on Law, reprinted in 1 The Works of James Wilson 408, 426 (1967).

17 4 The Debates in the Several State Conventions 113, 126, 127 (Elliott 1827).

18 Hamilton, The Federalist Papers, No. 65.

19 Id.

20 Joseph Story, 2 Commentaries on the Constitution, Impeachment Clauses, section 762 (1833).

21 Id.

22 Id., section 763.

23 Id., section 764.

24 U.S. Const., art. VI.

25 Charles Black, Impeachment: A Handbook (1974).

26 M. Farrand, 2 Records of the Federal Constitution of 1787, 551–52.

27 U.S. Const., amend. XII.

28 Story, 2 Commentaries on the Constitution, section 759.

29 U.S. Const., art. III, section 1.

30 United States v. Hastings, 681 F.2d 706, 711 (1982).

31 United States v. Claiborne, 727 F.2d 842 (9th Circuit 1984).

32 493 F.2d 1124 (7th Circuit 1974).

33 *Claiborne*, 727 F.2d at 709.

34 Id.

35 Id.

36 591 U.S. __ (2020).

37 U.S. Const., art. I, section 3, clause 7.

38 Trump v. Vance, 591 U.S. __ (2020).

39 U.S. Const., art. I, section 3, clause 7.

40 The judge was Thomas Porteous; the House impeached and the Senate convicted, removed, and disqualified him in 2010 for various offenses, including perjury on his Senate questionnaire.

41 Hastings v. Judicial Conference, 829 F.2d 91 (D.C. Cir. 1987).

42 U.S. Const., amend. V.

43 U.S. Const., art. I, section 3, clause 7.

2. THE IMPEACHMENT AND TRIAL OF ANDREW JOHNSON

1 David S. Heidler & Jeanne T. Heidler, Henry Clay: The Essential American 264 (2011).

2 Andrew Jackson, Speech, "April 15, 1834: Protest of Senate Censure."

3 Michael Holt, Attempts to Impeach John Tyler, American Heritage (February/March 2021).

4 Michael J. Gerhardt, The Forgotten Presidents: Their Untold Constitutional Legacy 55–57 (2013).

5 Michael J. Gerhardt, Lincoln's Mentors: The Education of a Leader 125 (2020).

6 Id. at 126.

7 Brenda Wineapple, The Impeachers: The Trial of Andrew Johnson and the Dream of a Just Nation 244 (2019).

8 60 U.S. 393 (1856).

9 Special Dispatches to the New York Times, Letter from Chief Justice Chase Relative to the Manner of Procedure, N.Y. Times, March 4, 1868; Walter Stahr, Salmon P. Chase: Lincoln's Vital Rival 575–576 (2022).

10 Wineapple, The Impeachers: The Trial of Andrew Johnson, at 292.

11 Id. at 296.

12 Id. at 299.

13 Id. at 303.

14 Stahr, Salmon P. Chase: Lincoln's Vital Rival, at 586.

15 Id.

16 Id. at 586–587. Chase knew most senators from having served in the Senate from 1849 to 1855 and other activities. In addition, Senator William Sprague of Rhode Island, who joined Chase for dinner on more than one occasion during the trial, was not only a fellow Republican but also Chase's son-in-law.

17 Myers v. United States, 272 U.S. 52 (1926). Chief Justice William Howard Taft, who had served previously as president of the United States, wrote the Court's majority opinion.

18 William Rehnquist, Grand Inquests: The Historic Impeachments of Justice Samuel Chase and President Andrew Johnson 271 (1992).

19 David O. Stewart, Impeached: The Trial of President Andrew Johnson and the Fight for Lincoln's Legacy (2010), at 284–299.

3. RICHARD NIXON AND WATERGATE

1 Andrew Kohl, From the Archives: How the Watergate Crisis Eroded Richard Nixon's Popularity, Pew Research Center, September 25, 2019, www.pewresearch.org/fact-tank/2019/09/25/how-the-watergate -crisis-eroded-public-support-for-richard-nixon.

2 U.S. v. Nixon, 418 U.S. 683 (1974), citing Marbury v. Madison, 57 U.S. 137, 177 (1803).

3 Id.

4 One of the two lawyers placed in charge of factual investigations was Bernard Nussbaum, who later served as Bill Clinton's first White House counsel.

5 Report by the House Judiciary Committee, Constitutional Grounds for Presidential Impeachment (1974).

6 House committee members who opposed Nixon's impeachment, after reading the report, ordered that a separate report be prepared to rebut the initial report's findings and conclusions.

7 Stephen Bates, Jack Goldsmith & Benjamin Wittes, The Watergate "Road Map" and the Coming Mueller Report, Lawfare, September 14, 2018.

8 Remarks of Congresswoman Barbara Jordan, "My Faith in the Constitution Is Whole; It is Complete; It Is Total," House Judiciary Committee, July 24, 1974.

9 This Day in History [August 9, 1974]: Nixon Resigns, History Channel. On October 17, 1974, President Gerald Ford took the unusual step of becoming the first president to testify in Congress in defense of a presidential action. In Ford's case, it was the pardon of Nixon that had caused Ford's own popularity to plummet. Ford did not take an oath before testifying, which further undercut his credibility on the issue. Ford's testimony that there was no "deal" or "agreement" between himself and Nixon to grant the pardon did not keep many of the members of the House Judiciary Committee from pressing him for answers on such matters as why he did not consult the special prosecutor, why did Ford not ask Nixon to admit his miscon-duct as a condition for the pardon, and whether Ford had any taped recordings of conversations with Nixon on the matter and if so whether those could be turned over to the committee.

David E. Rosenbaum, Ford Defends Pardon Before House Panel and Says There Was "No Deal" with Nixon, N.Y. Times, October 18, 1974.

10 Memorandum of the Deputy Attorney General, Presidential or Legislative Pardon of the President, August 5, 1974.

11 David Frost, Frost/Nixon: Behind the Scenes of the Nixon Interviews 254–56 (2007).

12 457 U.S. 731 (1982).

13 433 U.S. 425 (1977).

4. THE IMPEACHMENT AND TRIAL OF PRESIDENT BILL CLINTON

1 520 U.S. 681, 696–97 (quoting Youngstown Sheet & Tube Co. v. Sawyer, 343 U.S. 579, 634–35 (1952) (concurring opinion)).

2 Id. at 697.

3 Id. at 702.

4 Cass R. Sunstein, Impeaching the President, 147 U. Penn. L. Rev. 279, 280 (1998).

5 As the joint witness testifying before the House Judiciary Committee in 1998, I argued that a formal connection between an impeached official's misconduct and his duties was not required. Instead, I suggested, based on the history and practice of impeachment, that so long as the misconduct did serious damage to the nation and had a serious impact on a president's stature or ability to do his job then it would be a legitimate basis for impeachment, since it would seriously disable him from discharging his official duties.

6 Bruce Ackerman, The Case Against Lame Duck Impeachment (1999).

5. THE FIRST IMPEACHMENT AND TRIAL OF DONALD TRUMP

1 For a document making all these assertions, see Letter from the White House Counsel to Three House Committee Chairs, October 8, 2019.

2 Morrison v. Olson, 487 U.S. 654, 697 (1988) (Scalia, J., dissenting).

3 Patrick Cunningham, Gohmert Says Moms Shouldn't Send Kids to Harvard or Stanford Law Schools, KETK.com, December 5, 2019.

4 Michael J. Gerhardt, Testimony Before the House Judiciary Committee, Hearings on the Impeachment Inquiry into Donald J. Trump: Constitutional Grounds for Impeachment, December 4, 2019.

5 Pam Karlan, Hearing Before the House Judiciary Committee, The Impeachment Inquiry into President Donald J. Trump: Constitutional Grounds for Impeachment, December 4, 2019.

6 Kevin Breuninger, House Delivers Impeachment Articles to the Senate, cnbc.com, January 15, 2020.

7 Dershowitz Defamation Suit Against CNN Allowed to Proceed, bloomberglaw.com. May 26, 2021.

8 Peter Baker et al., Trump Fires Impeachment Witnesses Gordon Sondland and Alexander Vindman in Post-Acquittal Purge, N.Y. Times, February 7, 2020.

9 Christian Paz, All of Trump's Lies About the Coronavirus, The Atlantic, November 2, 2020.

6. DONALD TRUMP'S HISTORIC SECOND IMPEACHMENT AND TRIAL

1 Christina Wilkie, Trump Tries to Claim Victory Even as Ballots Are Being Counted in Several States—NBC Has Not Made a Call, cnbc.com, November 4, 2020.

2 Michael D. Shear & Stephanie Saul, Trump, in Taped Call, Pressured Georgia Official to "Find" Votes to Overturn Election, N.Y. Times, January 3, 2021 [updated May 26, 2021].

3 Mark Joyella, President Trump Tells Fox News He Worries About "the Country Having a President that Lost, and Lost Badly," forbes.com, December 13, 2020.

4 John Parkinson, After Suffering Personal Tragedy, Rep. Raskin Steps Up to Lead Prosecution of Trump, abcnews.go.com, February 9, 2021.

5 H. Res. 24, Resolution of Impeachment, January 13, 2021.

6 Senator Patrick Leahy of Vermont, Comment on Presiding Over the Impeachment Trial of President Donald Trump, January 25, 2021.

7 Emily Cochrane, Trifecta of Roles for Leahy: Witness, Juror and Judge in Trump's Trial, N.Y. Times, February 9, 2021.

8 Brakkton Booker, House Impeachment Managers Say Trump's "Incitement" Is Not Protected Speech, npr.org, February 10, 2021.

9 Salvador Rizzo, Trump Attorneys Falsely Claim He Was Denied "Due Process," Washington Post, February 13, 2021.

10 See Josh Blackmun & Seth Tillman, Is the President an "Officer of the United States" for Purposes of Section 3 of the Fourteenth Amendment?, 15 N.Y.U.J.L. & Liberty 1 (2021).

11 U.S. Const., amend. XXV.

12 Michael W. McConnell, How Democrats Could Have Made Republicans Squirm, N.Y. Times, February 18, 2021.

INDEX

ABOUT THE AUTHOR

MICHAEL J. GERHARDT is Burton Craige Distinguished Professor of Jurisprudence at the University of North Carolina at Chapel Hill and Scholar in Residence at the National Constitution Center. He is the author of six books, including *The Forgotten Presidents: Their Untold Constitutional Legacy*, which *The Financial Times* selected as one of the best nonfiction books of 2013. He has testified more than 20 times before Congress, and he served as special counsel to the Presiding Officer in the second impeachment trial of Donald Trump, and to the Chair and Ranking Member of the Senate Judiciary Committee for five Supreme Court nominations. He is one of only two legal scholars to testify before the House Judiciary Committee in two different presidential impeachment proceedings.